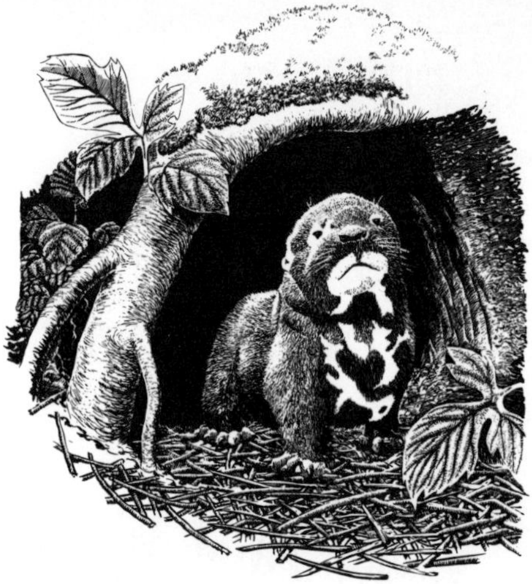

By the same author

BEEVER & COMPANY

500 ANIMALS FROM A TO Z

AND THEN THERE WERE NONE
(*with photographer Nina Leen*)

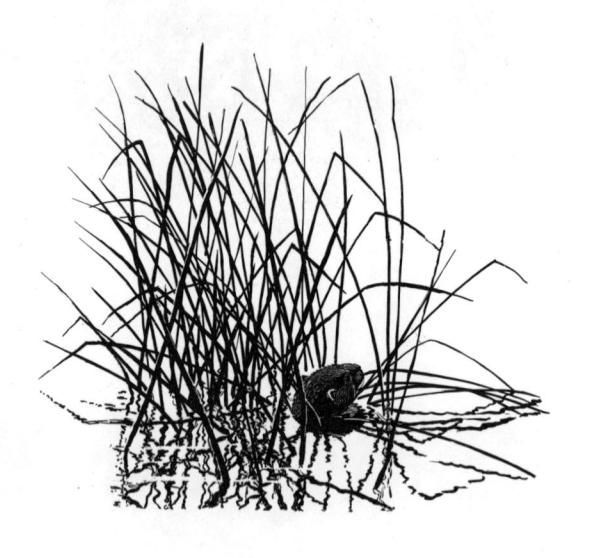

SAMAKI
The Story of an Otter in Africa

*A True-to-Life Novel
Written and Illustrated by*
J. A. DAVIS

E. P. DUTTON · NEW YORK

Copyright © 1979 by Joseph A. Davis
All rights reserved. Printed in the U.S.A.

No part of this publication may be reproduced or transmitted in any form or by any means, electronic or mechanical, including photocopy, recording or any information storage and retrieval system now known or to be invented, without permission in writing from the publisher, except by a reviewer who wishes to quote brief passages in connection with a review written for inclusion in a magazine, newspaper or broadcast.

For information contact:
E.P. Dutton, 2 Park Avenue, New York, N.Y. 10016

Library of Congress Cataloging in Publication Data

Davis, Joseph Anthony
Samaki: the story of an otter in Africa.
1. Hydrictis maculicollis or Lutra maculicollis—Legends and stories.
2. Otters—Legends and stories. 3. Mammals—Africa. I. Title.
QL795.O8D33   1979   599'.74447   78-9903
ISBN: 0-525-19601-3

Published simultaneously in Canada by
Clarke, Irwin & Company Limited, Toronto and Vancouver

Designed by Barbara Huntley

10 9 8 7 6 5 4 3 2 1

First Edition

For Jennifer,
who knew the real Samaki
and has grown up liking
otters, and
for Dorothy,
who liked them too.

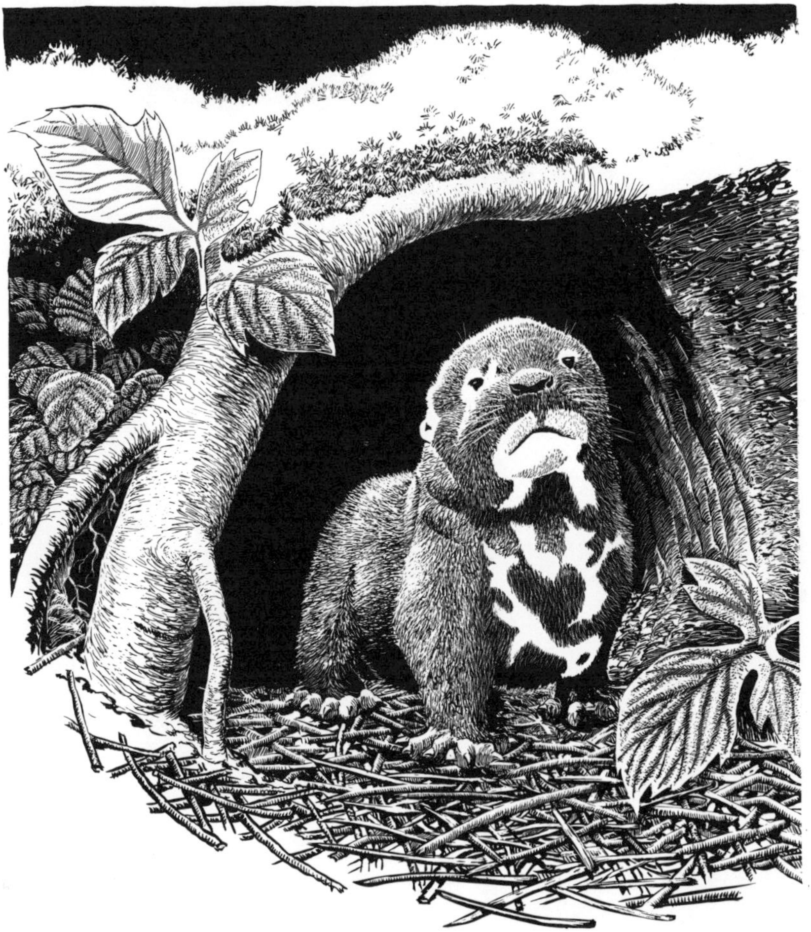

CHAPTER 1

He was ready to investigate the world outside. No, he wasn't quite ready. Yes, he was; he took a tentative step. And the moment Samaki's head emerged from the burrow into morning light the little otter took fright. The world was an overwhelming kaleidoscope of bright light and dark; unfamiliar sounds of birds and insects, leaves and twigs in the breeze, the soft moving of the river; the scents of green plants, of animals that had passed by, and flirting with him, almost hidden among the odors, a trace left by his mother the day before. Other than his mother's reassuring scent he could identify none of these new sensations, and their very strangeness upset him. Except for one timid approach to the entrance before, his world had been one of darkness, the medley of similar fragrances arranged at different places along his mother's body, her quiet sounds and gentle touches in the earthen womb that was the nest chamber.

But an eight-week-old otter cub has more curiosity than fear, even if it comes only in spurts, and Samaki took a forward step with his forepaw, leaving his hindfeet firmly planted, as if part of him wanted to go explore and part of him clung to the security of the familiar burrow. Then he took another step, again with a front foot, until he was stretched out as far as he could reach.

Splrrrrt! The spluttering sound was his own, but it would be hard to say whether he was more startled by the small bird whose close passage had pulled the sound from his throat or by the sound itself as it burst from within him. Nothing had ever so surprised him or his mother in the tranquility of the den; the cub had never before heard or used that explosive sound. His reaction to the sudden appearance of the swift, feathered blur had been more than vocal; Samaki's body had retreated at the same time toward the burrow. Then, the bird gone, the strength of curiosity reasserted itself, and Samaki was stretching out again. And perhaps unknown to a mind still immersed in a swarm of new sensory fascinations, the cub's hindfeet took a step each, to catch up with his forequarters. Haltingly he inched out again, pausing at every strange new sound, but pausing for less time with each repetition, until at last the two-syllable calls of the sunbird, perched some dozen yards away, and the rustling of leaves no longer seemed to hold menace. He turned to poke his nose at a yellowing leaf.

A small, olive frog arced away over the ground almost under the little otter's nose. He drew back in surprise; then, because the new thing was small, he bounded after it. In three hops the frog covered the gentle slope of the bank and plopped into the water, to lose itself in the mud. Samaki

was no longer surprised by anything this new toy did, and he kept going, down the bank, onto a sloping rock, until his head and forepaws were in the water.

Water! It was awful; it got into his nose. He snorted and choked, clearing his nasal passages as he retreated. Then he reached out a paw, tentatively, to touch this yielding new stuff, and the feel of it was odd. But the ripples that spread from his paw fascinated him—they were just near enough to see fairly clearly—so he stayed for a time just dabbling in the water. He had, of course, encountered water on his mother's fur when she returned from a hunt, but it had always been as droplets, at most, or mere dampness in her coat, something that was a transient part of her. This water before him was a thing in itself.

∽∽∽

Samaki was two months old, and his mind, as well as his body, had grown rapidly. He had been slightly the larger of the two cubs born to Maji in the den in that second week of September. Superficially they had looked like nondescript kittens fashioned by a Modigliani, longer in the neck than a kitten should be. Their eyes were sealed, and their low-set ears, at this age fleshy as the leaves of a sedum plant, had no external canals. Yet their tails, underdeveloped at birth, were oval in cross section, clearly the tails of otters, and their tiny paws were webbed and tipped with tightly curved, needle-sharp claws. The cubs were clothed in short grayish hair except for their chins and throats, which bore an indefinite pattern of white interrupted by peninsulas and islands of gray. They could lift their heads high almost from birth, and when they lost contact with their mother their shrill keening was strong. Each had been born wrapped in a short, tubular placenta that encircled him like a vest. Maji had quickly shorn each cub of his membranes, which she ate, and licked each clean of the amniotic fluid until his fur was dry. Although the mother otter had nipped the umbilical cords cleanly near each baby's abdomen, the vein in the smaller cub's umbilicus had failed to seal; bacteria entered, multiplied explosively, and in little more than a day the cub had died of the infection spread throughout his small body. The female had nosed the corpse, pushed at it, carried it in her mouth for a while, and then eaten the remains. It is not possible to say whether she did this deliberately to keep the den clean or whether it was a purely instinctive act, an escalation of the normal maternal grooming that came about when the cub failed to respond appropriately. Whatever the reason, Maji's actions kept a source of infection from spreading.

Maji spent less time out of the den hunting that night, her hunger lessened by the grisly meal. Thereafter she focused all her attentions on the surviving cub, Samaki. She slept curled about the baby, groomed him with delicate mincing nips of her incisors, and lay on her side, uppermost hindleg raised when he pushed his blunt muzzle into her groin to nurse.

For a long time the cub had seemed little more than an animated vegetable, sucking in nourishment at one end and extruding waste at the other, to be licked away by his mother. In the first days he urinated and defecated only in response to her warm tongue, but his excretory system soon found its own rhythm. His movements were almost all toward the warmth of fur and the source of milk, and if his mother shifted in her sleep and rolled away from him he called loudly.

On his twenty-fourth day Samaki's eyelids came apart, first at one corner, then during the next day completely. His eyes were flat and bleared, and his vision, had there been light to see by, would have been myopic in the extreme. The outer canals of his ears had perforated some time before. His coat had grown longer, lax, and the spotting on his throat was now distinct. He had been adding about an ounce a day to his three-ounce birthweight, and his rate of growth was increasing by the day. His whiskers, present when he was born, were lengthening. There were broad fans on either side of his muzzle, tufts over each eye and on each cheek behind the corners of his mouth, a tuft under his chin, and one on the lower aspect of each wrist. Each of these clusters of whiskers, or vibrissae, sent tactile information to the cub, at first as a means of locating his mother's mammary glands and later to warn of obstacles to his blind movements. As the whiskers grew longer, so did the cub's use of them grow more precise. No longer did he bump his head on the root that protruded into the den wall over him, and while his forward movement was still a kind of lurching, his wrist vibrissae warned him of a pebble or a depression.

For weeks the cub's life had been one mainly of snuggling, sleeping, and nursing. For now his tongue was broad and flat, and as he suckled it curled upward at the edges, sealing against his palate to form a tube that fit snugly around the nipple.

As he passed through the end of his seventh week, Samaki met pain for the first time in his brief life. The large, blade-flat carnassial teeth with which he would soon shear the flesh of his prey swelled within the gums of his upper jaws, forcing their way inexorably to the surface. The cub hurt. Suckling brought pain to his gums after only moments of the activity, and he nursed for only short periods, and more frequently, when he felt up to it. A lassitude settled upon him, too, and his occasional urges to chew, when he consummated them upon his mother's teat, drew punishing nips directed to the side of his muzzle, a sensitive spot. But the teeth cut through, the soreness subsided, and Samaki began to be his old self.

Two days ago Samaki had begun to become unusually restless. He had awakened at the feeling of his mother's movement in the den in the Kilindi River's bank. He had been sleeping pressed against her warm, soft side in the darkness, and her movement away from him disturbed and disappointed him. He had been hungry, too, and wanted to nurse, but dawn was near and Maji needed fish to soothe her own hunger and transmute into milk for her cub. She had been spending very little time in the river since the birth of the cubs; nor had she felt any desire yet to leave her surviving baby unprotected for longer than it took her to catch her food.

Samaki called after his mother in his high, piping chirp, the one that had so often brought her back for a reassuring touch. But this time she hadn't returned, even for a moment. He toddled down the burrow toward the entrance, following her scent and calling; but she was gone, and eventually he fell silent and returned to the nest chamber. There he flopped over on his back and began to play with a pebble. First he rolled it back and forth between his broad, rubbery webbed forepaws. Then he passed the toy backward and rolled it between the palm of his right front paw and the sole of the hindfoot on the same side. Then he let the pebble fall. It dropped to his plushy belly and rolled to the ground unnoticed, for the little otter had found something new to do. By rolling onto his side and curling his thick muscular tail forward, he found that he could clasp it with both hindfeet. And with equal suddenness he abandoned this latest form of the solitary play he had been inventing in the past weeks to fill the times when his mother was away. Until today, when playing grew dull, he would reach back, lying on one side, and pull his tail forward with his forepaws, to suck softly on the tip. It was somehow comforting, and he used to fall asleep, sucking with small tremors of his jaw, until he awoke again at Maji's warm touch. Sleeping with his mouth around his mother's teat was the most satisfying sensation to his drowsing mind, but like other mammals whose intelligence is highly developed he could invent a pacifier when the need arose; it was a very real need. Half a mile downstream another cub, Mkono, of the species called the clawless otter, lay on his back in his parents' den, sucking his paw. Almost webless, the pink doll-fingers, with vestigial nubs of claws that would one day disappear, fitted neatly into his broad mouth, index and little fingers to the sides of the canine teeth, the two middle fingers between them. Even as he sucked, his mother exhaled her souring breath, convulsively gasped in a lungful of river water, and drowned in the unyielding grip of a snare.

≈≈≈

Maji's holt had been excavated beneath an arching root a little distance above the edge of the river many lifetimes before her own. The original architect might have been an otter, or it might have been some small rodent, whose burrow was later enlarged by an otter. The second entrance, which emerged below the water, was without question an otter's handiwork, however, and generations of otters had occupied the holt almost continuously from its earliest days. Males had lived in it at times, and females at other times; cubs had drawn their first breaths in the quiet and darkness of its nest chamber, to be nursed and groomed, smelled but unseen, for a month or two by their mothers before being brought, or wandering on their own, through the twilight of the entranceway out into the light of sun or moon. Samaki knew his mother, in the early weeks, by the softness of her fur and the softer sound of her liquid, burbling voice. He knew the sweet-musky aromas of her coat and the smell of her breath when she came home each day, a smell that interested him, although he did not yet know that it was the lingering ghost of raw fish.

Today, when he found himself bored with the usual things he did while waiting for his mother's return, the cub had set out again toward the entrance, and today the world beckoned him. Earlier, when he had ventured near the entrance under the root, his eyes showed him nothing except a bright—blindingly bright—out-of-focus background and the blurry silhouette of the root framing it, with a few three-lobed leaves not far away. In the last few days the little otter's sight had improved somewhat, as it does with growth, and the world outside the den was beginning to take on more shape. Whether it was this slow improvement in his vision or just that Samaki's curiosity was growing along with his body, the outside world came to seem like an interesting place to be explored.

As he left the holt, he emerged under a carpet of lush moss which overhung the arching root on either side; a little way to the left ferns hung down. A narrow path of compacted stalks of the shed compound leaves of the tree above was devoid of living vegetation, but to either side grew patches of violets and other plants. Little more than two feet from the burrow's entrance the trail dropped a few inches over the edge of a slate-gray rock. Here the track divided, one spur running the remaining foot or so to the riverbank, hidden under a canopy of leaves; the other path turned left and wound along the bank downstream for several hundred yards. Mostly this trail passed beneath the concealing upland vegetation of the bank, but there were stretches where the bank was empty of tree and shrub, and some of these wore a carpet of green on either side of the trail; others were bare, their plant cover worn to oblivion by the lazy rubbing of otters' backs and flanks and bellies. A hundred yards from the den the bank grew lower and sloped more gently, and the bare earth, from which even old twigs and fallen leaves had been swept, marked one of Maji's principal hauling-out places. Beyond this point a few straggling plants strove for survival in the trail, where

Maji traveled less often. Other lesser creatures used the trail, too, but the wear of their traffic was insignificant compared with the section of track nearer Maji's holt.

Samaki had had enough of the water. He turned to the left and poked his way along, following the faint scent of his mother on the trail. Some eighty feet from the den he reached one of the bare patches, walled in on its far side by an extensive clump of reeds. The scuttling of a black beetle caught his eye just ahead, and he ambled over to nose at the insect.

A rustling in the greenery a few scant feet away froze him in midpoke; the reeds parted, and he found himself confronted by an animal. The creature was half again as big as Samaki and chunkier, with fur that was silvery gray above and brilliant white on its throat and cheeks. It was a cub of Africa's second otter species, the clawless otter—a true otter, but one whose build and hunting habits seem almost to have been inherited from a raccoon. It may well be, in fact, that clawless otters evolved their way of life and the anatomical modifications that accompany it just because the raccoon never reached Africa and that ecological niche lay waiting for some other species to exploit.

The clawless otter is a large species; the newcomer's father had weighed something over forty pounds, with a head and body that at three feet, were not much shorter than Samaki's father measured from nose to tail tip. The new cub's mother had been nearly as impressive, not much smaller than her mate. The species differs from the more typical otters in that its toes are not well webbed and its fingers scarcely at all. Cubs have small nubs of claws on all fingers and toes, but they lose them as they grow, except on the middle three toes of each hindfoot, where claws are needed for grooming and flea scratching. Perhaps more important in the long view, clawless otters pair more or less permanently, and the father participates in rearing the cubs, very likely from the moment of birth; spot-necked otter mothers, closer to the weasel stock from which otters evolved, treat males, including those who have fathered their cubs, with untempered ferocity until the cubs are several months old.

Mkono, the clawless cub, very nearly Samaki's age, was lonely. And he was hungry, too, but not desperately so, because his mother had already taken him grubbing for crabs and frogs along the shallows, and he had managed recently to find a few edibles. It had been two days since he had seen his parents, and little more than a day since hunger and loneliness had prompted his first excursions on his own from the den located along a brook that emptied into the Kilindi just upstream. When his mother had been caught in the snare, his father, still helplessly attending his dead mate, was clubbed to death by the returning trapper, who then skinned them both. Their hides were now drying in the sun in the village of Kijji; the carcasses, borne downstream, were being nibbled at by fishes of several kinds and, if they escaped the occasional snags in the river, would soon plummet over the falls, to be feasted upon by some of the few medium-sized crocodiles that still survived. The next thirty miles of river below the falls held only three of the big reptiles, which had been wary enough, or lucky enough, to escape hide hunters.

CHAPTER 2

Rooted where they were, the two young otters stared fixedly at each other with myopic eyes. Each uttered his *sotto voce* exhalation of mild alarm. From Samaki's mouth the sound was a low "Fff!"; from the clawless otter, a whispered "Hah!" To a member of his own species, the sound each had made would have been a warning signal instinctively understood, but their mutual anxiety had been expressed in different tongues, each meaningless to the other. Had either been a few weeks older he might have held his wary pose until a movement from the other sent him scurrying away. But these were two naive babes—in otter terms, still dry behind the ears.

As if at a signal the two cubs galumphed toward each

other, all caution forgotten. They fell upon each other, tumbling and rolling over the ground. Biting, each seized a broad mouthful of loose skin that gave in generous folds while the otter inside it twisted around as if he were floating un-

attached within a sack. This is how otter cubs play, no matter what species they are. And if the play seems ferocious, it's only because an otter's hide is very thick, tough, and loose, and the otter is not easily hurt. Once the larger cub bit down too forcefully, and Samaki twittered in pain; this cry was not a part of the clawless otter's inborn vocabulary, and while the sound interested him momentarily it carried no meaning, so he kept on biting. When the teeth, as they tightened their grip, began really to hurt, Samaki felt fear—his mother had never ignored a plea to stop a hard play-bite. Hurting more now, Samaki screamed—an awful, blood-chilling sound all otters make in desperation. This the other cub did understand. He understood, too, the savage bite Samaki aimed at him, even as he was loosening his grip. The cubs regarded each other for a moment, and then, as otters will, each forgot the pain and the play began anew.

Not far away in the river Samaki's mother, Maji, heard his scream, dropped the catfish she was eating on a flat rock, and plunged into the stream. She streaked homeward, most of the time underwater, where her speed was greater, surfacing intermittently for air and to listen for the scream again. When she reached the den through its underwater tunnel and found it empty, she exited through the second opening, where she found Samaki's scent trail. She passed the place where her cub had chased the frog. Pausing, she sniffed the area, but found none of the anal gland musk that would indicate this was where her cub had been frightened. Then she loped on again, ignoring the frog, which had come ashore again. A little farther along the bank she found Samaki, still wrestling with the clawless cub.

Maji rushed headlong toward the tumbling pair, upset to see a stranger, and worse, a stranger not of her own kind. With a barrage of bites, she sent the clawless cub bumbling off, then turned her attention to her own cub, nuzzling him as he pranced happily around her. She made no effort to pursue the other cub, so he waited not far away, wanting to rejoin Samaki, but afraid of the larger otter.

To save her cub from the danger his shriek had implied, Maji had interrupted her meal without eating enough, so she turned abruptly to scour the water for something more before bringing Samaki back to their den. As it happened, the cub was about the right age to learn how to swim, although the female knew this only on a level below her consciousness, if she knew it at all. Before she had pushed more than once with her webbed feet, she surfaced, turned and called to her son in the high, birdlike chirp that had almost always brought him back to the nest chamber when he sought to explore the burrow. Samaki heard and tried to follow, but he hesitated at the edge of that surface that couldn't be stepped on. He got his forepaws wet, stopped, and called back to his mother. But instead of coming to him she dove under the surface and disappeared from sight. Samaki yearned to go looking for her, but she was gone, and the water held no trail of scent for him to follow. And when he tried to sniff at the water it filled his nose.

Without warning, almost under his stinging nose, his mother's head broke through the surface, wreathed in large, silver bubbles. At first he was terrified to see her disembodied head, but before the fright registered fully her burbling voice dissolved the fear. So, happy to be reunited, the cub sprang forward, plunged into the water, and was baptized. Water got into his nose. Water got into his ears. Water got into his fur. Wetness, even for an otter, is an acquired taste, and this cub had yet to acquire it. He turned to run back out of the water and, without quite knowing he was doing it, swam clumsily to the bank. His mother swam away and dived again, leaving a soggy, unhappy little otter standing on the bank in a growing puddle, calling frantically.

On her way to the deep water where fish were to be found, Maji's urge to hunt snuffed itself out, to be replaced by a stronger need. She doubled back and scrambled ashore to the place where her cub stood, still trying to clear his nostrils. She touched him briefly with her nose, a reassuring contact; then, with no preamble, she grasped the skin of his cheek firmly in her teeth and hauled him bodily into the river. Freed in the water, he hurried toward the bank, unaware that this time he had closed the muscular valves in his nostrils and ears and kept the water out. But even before he had a firm foothold on the river's edge, he was grasped again, this time by the scruff of the neck, and hauled into the water again. And again. And again. Maji grabbed her cub by any convenient part of his head and neck—by the jowl, the ear, the throat—and took him forcibly into the

river until the compulsion left her and she turned her attention to resuming the hunt.

In minutes she broke the surface again near the cub. In her absence she had eaten a small fish, and now, twitching between her jaws was a catfish. She came ashore and dropped her booty in front of her son. What a wonderful toy it was! It flopped when Samaki reached out a paw to touch it. He lurched forward and pressed the paw onto it. When it began to flop again, it reminded him of his mother's foot those times when he had wrestled with it and nipped it playfully.

Back in the den he used to clutch at her foot with both paws and pretend to bite fiercely, so he grasped the fish in the same way and began to bite. An otter has tough, thick skin, though, and Samaki's first playful bite passed deep through the soft skin of the fish. The taste of the juices in his mouth was odd, but not at all unpleasant; it recalled the scent he'd noted on his mother's mouth after her absence. He bit a piece from the fish's middle, tilted his head upward, and chewed. If he noticed his mother slip away again, Samaki was too much immersed in his new experience to care. While he was still engrossed in savoring his first solid food, the female returned, this time with a larger fish. Samaki turned his attention to the new fish, and while he played at eating its softer parts his mother finished the smaller one. In time the cub lost interest in this new food and bumbled off to chase a grasshopper while his mother ate most of what was left of the fish. By now the sun was higher in the sky; Maji led her son back to the den, pulling him by the jowl when he dawdled.

When they were gone, the clawless otter cub crept from his hiding place. He waddled over to the remains of the fish and hungrily finished it off. The small crab he had found earlier had not been enough for one meal. Then, feeling more comfortable, he found a rotting hollow stump and stretched out inside it for a nap.

Samaki passed the day with his mother in the den. He nursed from time to time and slept much of the time, sometimes with the female's teat in his mouth and her foot resting lightly on his head, sometimes apart from her. He awoke at intervals, restless to explore the world outside, but always his mother awoke from her light sleep to call him back or, failing that, to pursue and drag him back to the nest by whatever part of his head or neck was handy. As always, the cub's meek response to these indignities was to go limp and be moved like some inanimate thing.

Late in the afternoon hunger urged Maji to wakefulness. This time she left the den through the tunnel that opened under the water, and when the cub followed her down the tunnel she made no attempt to stop him. She slunk along the low, downsloping passage and disappeared into the unsubstantial floor at its end. Samaki called after her, but there was no answer. At the first feel of the water, Samaki recognized it; without a semblance of conscious effort, he inhaled, closed his nostrils and ears, and thrust his head below the surface to look for her. In the twilight of the water-filled burrow he saw nothing, but he had established an automatic response to the fluid that would soon be as much his world as the land. The small muscles associated with his nose and ears would nevermore fail to squeeze shut the openings when he prepared to swim, and water would henceforth be a milieu of pleasure only. Only one obstacle now stood between the otter and his birthright to be an expert swimmer: the fear of not being able to touch ground. And before nightfall his mother would see to it that he overcame the fear.

Samaki's mother had not really gone away; she had risen to the surface to make certain no danger was about, and having satisfied herself, dove again toward her den. The cub was dipping his head repeatedly now, more intrigued by the cool feel of the water that no longer caused him to choke. A dark form blotted out the weak light in the underwater passage, and his mother's nose gently bumped against his. Samaki withdrew his head and the adult squeezed out of the water. The burrow was a tight fit, and Samaki had to back up to avoid being wedged against the wall. The female pressed on toward the den, backing her son along the tunnel until he remembered to turn his small, supple body and lollop along in the van. Near the den Samaki's mother turned at the fork that led to the dry exit; Samaki had continued toward the den, realized he was alone, chirped loudly, and doubled back to follow Maji on her new course.

The air had a different smell and feel as the cub neared the end of the burrow. A fine drizzle, the vestige of the short rains of October, dampened the air and filled it with a muted whisper. Maji paused at the opening, checking for traces of danger, and moved out into the rain. For Samaki, leaving the safety of the holt suddenly seemed unattractive, as it had earlier in the day, more so because of the added sound of the precipitation. His first step outside put his head into the drizzle; the new tactile sensation fed his uneasiness, and he withdrew. Maji, looking back over her shoulder, called to him, but the cub lay anxiously within the tunnel. His mother returned impatiently and hauled him bodily from his shelter. She loosed him some dozen steps away, when he began to move along with her on his own feet, and by this time the fine droplets no longer bothered him. Reassured by Maji's presence, he bounded off at her heels.

The otters traveled along the water's edge for a distance, but their progress was slow, as Samaki dawdled to poke at scuttling beetles and emerging worms. Before long they were at their destination, a place where the water lay only a few inches deep over a submerged shelf of the river bed. Here Maji waded into the water; her cub followed, but very slowly, picking up each paw carefully and stopping often to practice his newly learned trick of holding his breath, poking his head under the surface.

Soon Samaki was behaving as naturally in the shallows as he did on land, investigating the water's treasures and, more important, holding his breath without conscious effort whenever his attention turned to something underwater. Once, while he poked at a small snail on the shelf, Maji drew near and nipped at him playfully. Just as he did in the den, Samaki recognized the pinch as an invitation to a wrestling match; he responded by rearing back a little and pouncing. Mother and cub rolled and tumbled in the shallow water, the tempo of their writhing increasing steadily, as the billow of churned mud spread around them and drifted almost imperceptibly in a lazy eddy. Their frenzied play spun them in fits and starts toward the edge of the shelf and over into the deeper water of the channel.

So absorbed in the tussle was Samaki that some time passed before he realized the ground was no longer under his feet. He looked down and saw only the hazy suggestion of waterweeds swaying below him, and he panicked. The first time in its life that a terrestrial animal loses the reassuring feel of solid ground beneath it brings the terror of disorientation; even an otter must give up this sense of security before he can know the exultation of mastering the water's three dimensions. Thrusting his head again into the air, Samaki saw his mother a little way distant, and, frantic, he tried to run to her. But this was the river. The churning of his four webbed paws got him nowhere. Each return sweep of a foot canceled the forward motion of the last backward thrust, and his efforts only raised him a little higher in the water, jiggling back and forth. But even in his fear the little otter's muscles were learning new patterns, and as automatically as he had perfected the means of shutting water from his nose, Samaki discovered there was a way to let the paws go limp as they drew forward, so as not to push against the water, and to spread his fingers and toes stiffly on the backward push, to thrust strongly against the element. The ordinary postural adaptations of terrestrial locomotion served to alter direction in the river, too. By imperceptible degrees the cub found himself moving toward his mother. It was an awkward dog paddle, but it was work-

ing. Maji treaded water, keeping just outside his reach, and led him, swimming better with each stroke, back to the shelf. When his feet again met the mud, it almost didn't matter anymore. Almost.

Standing elbow-deep on the shelf, breathing hard from his exertions, and nuzzling his mother, Samaki hadn't yet noticed that the rains were over.

It was time to eat. Maji wheeled about and melted into the deep water again. The cub called to her anxiously. He peered out across the river, seeking the rounded, blackish head, but he saw nothing. He splashed out of the water, up onto the sloping bank, to scan again from a higher vantage point. As he did, from around an upstream boulder there drifted an object. His heart began to race with recognition, then with alarm, for it was not his mother's head, but an elongated, grayish, rough thing.

"Ffff!" He hung somewhere between suspicion and alarm. "Ffff!" He arched his neck, then lowered it and stretched it forward to the limit, shifting from side to side, to see from different angles.

"Ffff!"

He backed up a few steps as the small log floated past at the near edge of the channel and tried to stand upright on his hindlegs. Still too young to manage the posture, Samaki fell over, now really frightened because his falling seemed somehow caused by the strange object and because he was, for all too long an instant, vulnerable. The log drifted past harmlessly, but another response had established itself. The otter's unease when faced with the unfamiliar and his outright fear of large floating things came to him unlearned, but in reacting under its influence he had added something to it. The same piece of wood, met with on land, would evoke mild curiosity, but in the water it might have been a crocodile, the only predatory being to represent a constant threat to the otters of Africa during their evolution. Pythons and large carnivores are infrequent sources of danger, from whom the river offers haven, but crocodiles may appear anywhere, silently and insidiously, and instinct has primed the otter to detect them.

CHAPTER 3

Swimming and diving are separate skills. Samaki could now maneuver with reasonable skill at the surface of the river, but its bottom, in all but the shallowest water, lay as unreachable to him as the vault of the sky. Below him he could see, and see more sharply than in air, the moving forms of fish and crabs and patches of undulating waterweeds, but they moved beyond his grasp. He was the prisoner of buoyancy. He could watch below him with fascination, and sometimes with dismay, when his mother's dark form sped downward; but when the cub tried to follow, nothing worked. He would duck his head, arch his torso, and kick as hard as he could, but always it ended the same way—he would find himself hanging at the surface, doubled over, thrashing. Whether his baby's fur was too effective in retaining air or his bones not yet solid enough, Samaki was bound to the river's roof. Or it may have been only that he had yet to learn the strength of the kicks that would sunder, thrust by momentary thrust, the upward pull of the water.

But one evening the necessary knack manifested itself. The triumph was unbearably brief. There he was, standing on his nose, half his tail arched upward in the still air—and then his rump bobbed helplessly upward and he floated at the surface again. Samaki dove again, and this time, heaving with both hindfeet spread like fans, he descended in two spurts toward his mother before he popped up again, kicking the air. Maji saw her son struggling, as she glided just above the bottom. In an instant she streaked upward, outracing her chain of bubbles, to nuzzle his chest and breach at his side. In his excitement, Samaki pounced on her. In the tussle he forgot about the challenge he had begun to meet. When next he remembered the bottom, his movements were stronger and better coordinated. Before they returned to the holt the cub could follow Maji on short forays below the surface.

That night Maji was awakened by spasmodic kicking: Samaki was diving in his dreams. She stirred, removed herself a little, as far as the nest chamber would allow, and began to nibble absently at the fur of her hip. A muffled sound stopped her. Something was in the burrow.

Like a snake, Maji flowed over herself and dashed into the tunnel.

"Ffff!"

The footfalls halted. She drew a sharp breath through her nostrils, and the breath carried a trace of male scent.

"Ffff! Ffff!" The anxious aspiration came louder from her, picking up a rasping quality, rougher in texture, until it was the splutter of anxiety pushed to its limit. The otter made no further move. Behind her, Samaki spluttered in his sleep, his experience with the floating log rekindled by his mother's sound, and then was quiet again.

Still no sound of movement from the intruder. Maji arched her neck involuntarily and growled, a low, nasal, whining growl, like the sound of a distant sawmill. She growled again. The musk of the male still filled her nostrils.

There was no further preamble; the mother, in defense of her cub, hurtled toward the interloper intent on drawing blood. But the male was already in flight, awkwardly backing toward the forest outside. One of her canines gouged his fleshy upper lip before he was quit of the burrow, and once in the open he whirled around and was gone. Maji's jaws slammed shut on the air inches from his tail.

~~~

The Mazingira is one of East Africa's lesser rivers. It arises, in mountains that are less than spectacular, as a complex of swift-flowing streams that work their turbulent way downward to feed larger tributaries like the Kilindi. These empty their contents of water and silt into the Mazingira, and after many miles of slow, broad idling and occasional plunging cataracts, it, in turn, discharges itself into a freshwater lake of a size rarely encountered on any continent. Although the Mazingira is not a major river, it flows throughout the year, managing a perceptible flow even in times of drought.

Mto had lived on the Mazingira River for five years, a long time for an otter. Like others of his kind, he had relocated his principal holt several times, and the boundaries of his elongate territory had shifted several times. They had shrunk inward as new males established themselves along the adjacent stretches of river, and expanded when the incumbents were removed by disease, accident, predator, or old age. At the west end of his territory, downstream, lived a truculent male whose meeting meant a squabble at best. Their common boundary shifted occasionally, but it was normally well defined. Mto's upstream neighbor, perhaps a half brother born to a later mating, was of a more amiable temperament. Their infrequent encounters were friendly and playful outside the breeding time, and a reciprocated tolerance resulted in a stretch of river shared by the two. Mto claimed, as well, a two-mile stretch of the Kilindi River, where that tributary met the Mazingira within its domain. No male neighbor had lived on the Kilindi for nearly a year, since the last one died in his den of a runaway infection begun by the bite of a pouched rat he had attempted to kill.

Mto's territory overlapped the home ranges of two females, one of them Maji, who denned principally on the

Kilindi. With these he had a casual, but friendly, relationship over much of the year. Meeting one of the females, he would indulge with her in a two-sided bout of sniffing of the face and genital regions; the pair would almost invariably sport in the water and on the bank, wrestling and nipping with restraint, for upward of an hour before each resumed the private business of the day.

Occasionally a female met his greeting with a shrill rebuke, and if her antagonism proved more persistent than his sociability, the big male would take his leave voluntarily. He had never returned an angry stab, and his departure was always genuinely nonchalant.

As is usual for an otter, Mto enjoyed companionship. The occasional female rebukes were usually a sign of the onset of the breeding season, and when a female was in heat Mto's sexual urgings grew strong enough to override his insouciance. At these times his persistence in the face of even a prolonged, and sometimes savage, rejection was boundless and heroic. After some days of his single-minded attention, all but the most intractable females tolerated his advances and at the height of the estrus became willing mates. As their ardor waned, they would become difficult again, and his concentrated pursuit would come to be interrupted by small distractions of many kinds, until at last the lure of bachelor life pulled him back into his old routines. Later the females would be cordial, but sexually uninteresting, companions again, to be met with as his travels allowed.

On his last few patrols Mto had failed to detect any trace of the pair of clawless otters with whom he had shared his stretch of the Kilindi. Although their den was on a smaller tributary, the Kijito, they occasionally worked the

Kilindi along the far reaches of his territory. Each species treated the other with wary respect, kept its distance, and shared the resources of the habitat. The larger otters grubbed in the shallows, where their chief prey consisted of crabs, molluscs, and other invertebrates; they took a few fish, but not enough to be competitors with the spot-neck. He, in turn, ate an occasional small crab, but concentrated in the main on swifter creatures. Now their scent grew stale, replaced by that of a cub of their species. Mto noted that the new scent lacked the richness of the older ones; he was aware that something had changed, but was unconcerned.

Mto was large for his species, some forty-two inches from tip to tip, and he weighed sixteen pounds. He had less spotting than most other otters in the region, with only a few small blotches on his throat. On the left side of his muzzle the white upper lip was marked with a dark "beauty spot." He was sleek, with a hint of a bull neck; in the base of his tapering tail lay a thick deposit of fat, evidence that he had been feeding well and was in robust health.

Twice since Samaki's birth, the old male had run afoul

of Maji. Once, she had been devouring a fish on the bank, wolfing it down as speedily as she could so as to return to her maternal duties. She had spluttered at him explosively, lunged at him so vehemently that his retreat had been anything but casual. More recently, he had gone part way down the burrow before he had been met by a fury, and he had backed out hastily, with a pinched lip that was sore for several days after. But cub scent had hung in the air of the burrow, and Mto's curiosity was high.

The moon had passed through two full cycles since Mto's last rout. He had lived long enough to know that Maji's hostility would last a while. And yet with time the desire to see her again grew, and he remembered the smell of the cub. One other time he had followed the trail of mother and son along the bank, but when he heard their returning footfalls he slipped quietly into the river and was off. On the trail, Maji detected her mate's scent, stiffened, listened intently, and continued, staying close to her cub and dragging him when he began to dawdle. It is widely held that the males of most members of the weasel family will kill their offspring, given the opportunity, and Maji's anxiety gave evidence that instinctively she concurred. Mto, in fact, had been moved by curiosity and nothing more. He might indeed have killed or injured a younger Samaki out of clumsiness, and it had probably been best that Maji drove him off while the cub was tiny; but that danger had ceased when her cub became ambulatory. If the protective feelings of female spot-necked otters for their cubs had diminished during the time the males' paternal instincts were evolving, the rearing of young might have been easier. But evolution moves in spurts, sometimes without coordinating its effect on the sexes. In the case of the late pair of clawless otters that had lived along the Kilindi tributary, the species had already developed a more or less permanent bonding of pairs, and the male's solicitousness for his offspring had arisen accompanied by a mellowing of the female's attitude. But the spot-necked otters have not yet achieved this felicitous state, and perhaps the species never will.

∾∾∾

By mid-January, Samaki was five months old and a veteran of nearly three months of swimming, running, and wrestling with his mother. His coordination had increased phenomenally. He had grown adept at catching frogs and small invertebrates and had even managed a few times to capture one of the slower fish.

The sun had not yet risen above the trees. The river still wore its soft mantle of mist, rising in wisps of dull silver against the deep shadows of the trees. Maji and Samaki were already searching for breakfast, and the cub had just surfaced after narrowly missing a small *Barbus*. As he scanned the envelope of fog, looking for his mother, a dark head broke the surface a few feet away. Samaki dove and surfaced next to the approaching otter, but when he pressed his nose against its muzzle the scent was wrong. The larger animal looked wrong, too, with its spot on the upper lip. But it nuzzled him back and continued to nuzzle, at his ear, his neck, shoulders and flank, and then under the base of his tail. By then Samaki had begun to respond in kind, and the two otters floated lazily, their mutual inspection continuing without haste. A third head, Maji's, moved toward them, nosed Samaki perfunctorily, and turned toward Mto. She nosed him briefly, then burbled a low, affectionate greeting, leaped upon him, and the two began wild, happy gyrations that sent the tatters of mist dancing. Samaki could not tolerate a spectator's role, and before the adults had barely begun, the writhing knot had three dangling, lashing ends.

For Maji the time of reconciliation had come.

CHAPTER 4

The male otter's companionship embraced both mother and cub equally, at least when Samaki was awake. But the little otter tired easily in these days of vigorous play with two adult companions; his endurance would grow over the ensuing weeks, but for the moment, grownups were taxing playmates. Samaki broke off his sport often to rub himself on a rock and lapse into sleep. Drowsiness never crept up on him, but came as an imperative demand. The adults went on with their revels without him, although Maji returned to him at frequent intervals to touch him with her nose before rejoining the male.

The otters were abroad for longer periods now, and

they were ranging farther from the home den. They slept in some of the lesser holts along the stream, sometimes all three together; and sometimes Mto left for a den of his own. Once, the three moved into a holt of Mto's.

February brought a change in Maji. Her solicitude for her son remained, enriched by a growing affection for him as an individual, an affection that would endure when the irresistible urgings of motherhood had faded; but at times she found the old male irritating. With increasing frequency she answered his attentions with chittering threats and an occasional nip. Her moods came and went with the suddenness of the last season's rain squalls; Mto paid them as much heed.

She was drying herself on a broad, sloping rock in the river. The smooth, polished stone darkened as it absorbed water in microscopic pores, spilling the excess back into the river; the sun pulled additional moisture from her coat. Mto, idling in the water nearby, approached, reached up his head, and nuzzled her neck. Maji chittered and struck at his face; he sank below the surface. Minutes later the male ambled up onto the rock and nosed her again, to be repulsed once more. He was standing next to her, and when Maji struck he rolled slowly over onto his side, draping himself diagonally across her form. For reasons that only an otter may know, this drained Maji of her hostility, and when, after a while, Mto arose, she accepted his invitation to swim.

Maji's changes of mood increased in frequency by the day. And then, a week or two later, her bouts of hostility nearly ceased. She and Mto began to spend long periods floating in the river, the male clasping her around the shoulders. They were mating, and when a curious Samaki swam over to join the game, he found himself, for the first time in his life, totally ignored. A young otter in a playful mood is difficult to ignore, but so intent were the male and female that even when the cub scrambled up onto their coupled torsos, causing them to sink lower into the water, they were oblivious. Faced with the two unresponsive guardians, Samaki's attention began to wander. A leaf, drifting on the current, caught his eye. He left the two to their embrace and raced after the leaf as if it were the swiftest and craftiest of prey. Snap! He held it tightly between his teeth. Diving with it, he released the leaf and maintained his depth, watching its slow rise to the surface. Then he fell upon it again, clasping it between the broad webs of his forepaws.

Again and again he attacked the leaf and released it for another capture.

The form of a fish glittered below him. The leaf, tattered by now, swirled in the slight turbulence left by the cub, who was now streaking toward the fish. The chase was short; Samaki surfaced and, treading water with his hindfeet, held the small body in his forepaws. It took two bites to consume the fish. Then Samaki remembered the adults.

Neither acknowledged his approach. He nuzzled, first his mother, then the male, but neither returned his greeting;

nor did either one rebuke him. Samaki left them again, this time to explore the far side of the river.

The exploration of the far bank had not been very profitable. A grasshopper had catapulted itself out of sight into tall grass before Samaki had even come close. There had been a few small beetles, but the last had left an unbearably disagreeable taste in his mouth which only the river water could undo. So the little otter was swimming again, slowly, underwater, nosing along the bank, hoping for a frog. He rounded a large rock protruding from the water, here and there probing the mud with his nose; he half expected the sudden flight of some small water insect to brush against his sensitive whiskers, triggering a quick dart of his head that would make it his.

Above, in the still backwater in the lee of the rock, dozens of small, elliptical silhouettes traced slow arabesques on the surface. Whirligig beetles, similar to those found in the northern continents, seem to spend most of their active time describing little circles and curls on the water film. Occasionally they climb out on exposed twigs or stones, and from time to time one dives below its reeling companions to search the water's bottom for the edible bodies of dead insects. Each of the whirligig's two compound eyes is divided into two seemingly separate eyes, one looking above the surface, one below. Samaki watched for a moment from near the bottom. But he was being watched, as well, and when he kicked upward into the midst of the circling beetles, the dancers scattered before he broke the surface, only to regroup a few feet away. A new game, and it occupied the young otter for some minutes, during which time he managed to engulf only one beetle. But it was the game that mattered; in little time Samaki perfected the knack of herding the beetles by attacking one flank of the group. In the course of his play he moved the whirligigs a few yards upriver toward a sparse patch of short reeds, and here he lost interest in them, for here, in the reeds, his activity set into motion a larger and more interesting creature—a crocodile hatched far downriver the year before.

Last June, after some three months of maternal protection, the reptilian brood had broken up, each young one setting out on its own, to pass through the sieve of river life, where storks, fish, and larger crocodiles would remove most of them from the competition at a tender age. Those that survived the natural hazards would grow large enough to become targets for human hunters. Few would survive to pass their genes to another generation, and fewer still would achieve their potential growth. The scarcity of large crocodiles on the Mazingira and its tributaries was, in fact, the result of man's greediness for their hides. And because of this scarcity, the river supported a greater number of otters than it had in centuries past.

The fleeing crocodile measured a little less than two feet. She was just about as long as the otter, but her bulk was less. Samaki regarded her warily, for something about the saurian shape touched his inborn fear. Yet, she was hurrying away, and his predatory instinct was aroused. More sinuous than any fish's, the lashing, plated tail demanded his attention; almost of their own accord, Samaki's feet spurred him to pursuit. The otter overtook the crocodile easily, and by luck his first bite pierced the scaly hide of the reptile's neck. Sharp mammalian teeth crushed muscle and sinew and bone in the first snap. The crocodile continued to writhe, tail whipping spasmodically, jaws gaping and seeking a hold; but Samaki had her by the neck and now clasped her with all four paws. The crocodile was dead, but the reality and finality of that state had not yet been made known to her tissues. Two quick bites severed the head completely, but for the tough hide of the throat, from which it dangled, swaying loosely. Even at this size a crocodile is as much prey as predator, and the otter is the superpredator of the waters, to whom other species are food; only after it achieves a length of three or four feet does a crocodile displace the otter at the top of the chain of the eaten and the eaters. But even at two feet the crocodile might have been the victor; had she clamped her jaws on the otter's throat, close enough to his head to render his own jaws useless, it might have been the reptile who would dine. But

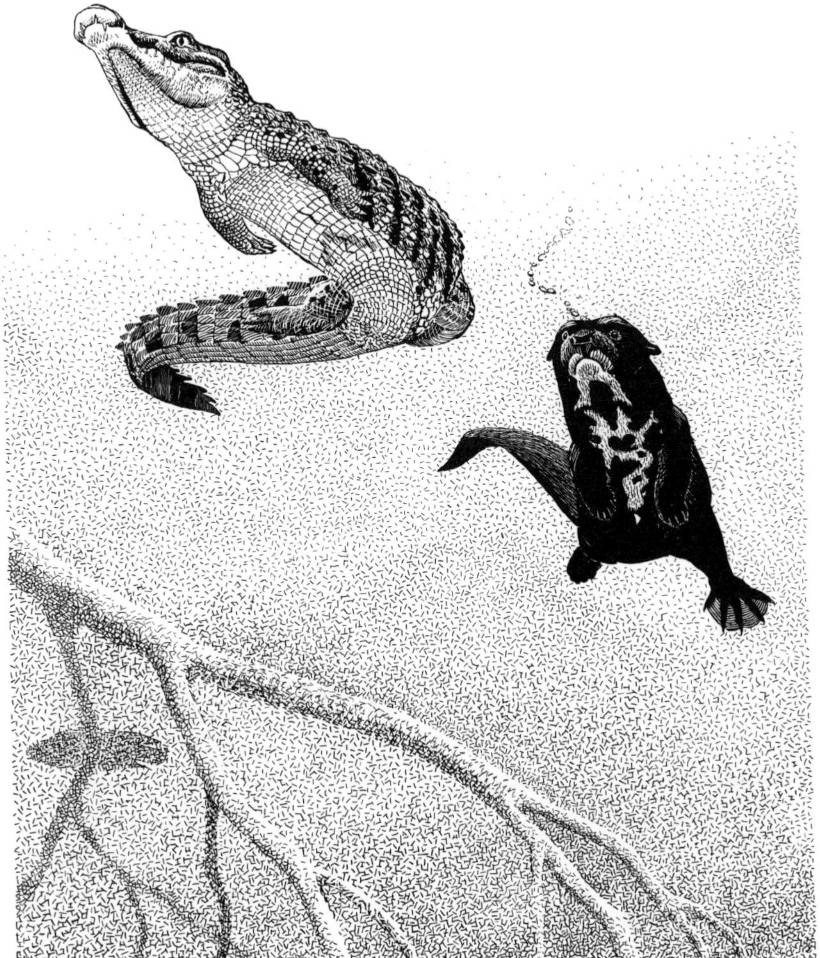

she would certainly not have played with her inanimate meal first.

Samaki released the body; it hung before him, barely buoyant now that its lungs had lost their contents, and then began to drift upward almost imperceptibly. Samaki reached out with his right paw and nudged it to the left. When it had moved a few inches, he glided under it, belly up, and pulled it to his chest. He clasped it again and bit once more, freeing the head and pitching upward in a languorous arc. Surfacing only to refill his lungs, the otter spent long minutes below the surface executing his sensuous pavanne. But in time he tired of the movement, grasped the carcass firmly in midtrunk, and swam with it to the bank, where he hauled it out and sampled its taste. The skin was tough, but no match for the knifeblades of his carnassial teeth, and he ate about a third of the body.

His mother! It was time to seek her out again.

Maji and Mto were sprawled under a low bush not far from where he'd left them, the male stretched out on his back, the female, a few feet away, curled like a sleeping tabby. Samaki searched the bank until he picked up the adults' scent, followed it, and uttered the piping chirp that said, "Where are you?" Maji answered, rising to her feet; they met just outside the sheltering shrub, and before they had ended the ritual of nuzzling Mto was there to repeat the ceremony. Formalities over, Samaki leaped upon his father, nipping and clasping, pushing and worrying his loose skin, and himself being pushed, nipped, worried, and rolled on the earth. When the playing spent itself, the two returned to the shade, where Maji had already retreated and fallen asleep. On the other bank of the river, some distance away, the remains of the young crocodile were already beginning to spoil in the heat of the sun and would soon attract carrion beetles, which would laboriously work it below the ground if a passing marabou stork didn't find it first.

Midday found the otters in a little-used holt nearby, where they slept again until early evening. Maji chittered angrily in her sleep twice, and Mto, himself asleep, stiffened slightly. When she awoke Maji was again cordial, and the otters repaired to the river to hunt.

The three otters hunted separately. Each of the adults ate its own fish, but each suffered Samaki to partake of the booty, a few mouthfuls at least, before he managed to bring off a successful catch himself. Sated, the otters moved off to defecate, but Maji eliminated in the river, a practice she had assumed occasionally since coming into heat. Mto plunged into the water, investigated the floating mucoid stool briefly, and approached the female. She hung upright for a moment, chittered at him, struck once, and succumbed to his ardor. Samaki took his cue and set out again to explore.

The uneaten parts of the crocodile already had a distasteful odor. He shook his head and moved on in the rapidly waning light. There in the shadow of the trees the darkness was already deeper than even his sensitive eyes could penetrate; he turned again toward the bank, where the sky over the water still provided light. A little way more and the bank became a gentle slope. Ahead of him a clawless otter grubbed in the muddy sand of the shallows. Samaki halted. He reared up on his hindlegs, a posture he had by now almost mastered, peered intently at the animal, listened, and searched for a scent. He had never seen an adult clawless otter, so he had no way of knowing that this otter was far from grown. A memory, half-formed, tantalized him for an instant, swelling, taking shape, like the bud on a shrub, until it blossomed, unfolded, and once again in his mind he saw and smelled Mkono. Samaki dashed ahead. He had known only Mkono, and it never occurred to him that this might be another otter, whose response to the onrush might be unpleasant. Yet something deeper than consciousness halted him midway, and he stopped and uttered a chirp. The second otter had already turned at Samaki's footfalls, alert and ready to flee. He recalled his early play with the cub, Samaki, but he remembered, too, the attack of Samaki's mother, and in the time since, on several occasions when he had encountered Mto, the big otter had kept his distance. Mkono hesitated.

Samaki chirped again. Mkono advanced uncertainly, and the spot-neck followed suit. They were now less than a body length apart, sniffing for a familiar scent. Mkono, who was starved for the companionship a young otter needs so badly, made the first real move. He launched himself at Samaki, bowling him over. Something in the feel of the other's body and limbs identified him, and Samaki responded as before with a lively tussle that rolled them about on the bank, crashing into small bushes and crushing grass and herbs beneath them. Neither uttered a sound, save the occasional complaint against a hard bite in a sensitive place. But a more thin-skinned observer, seeing jawfuls of skin pulled out from a distorting face until it seemed they would tear free, would have winced at the vigor of the play. Yet the play went on interminably before Samaki's stomach interrupted. He broke free, releasing his own grip on Mkono simultaneously, and trotted toward the water. The clawless cub peered over his shoulder questioningly, but quickly got to his feet and shambled to the water, too, remembering the morsels he had been searching for when his companion arrived on the scene. By the time Samaki had caught and eaten a small catfish, Mkono, too, had dined. The clawless cub was making his way to a cavity beneath a riverside tree

root when Samaki returned, and the smaller cub followed him to the den. Somehow the two managed to fit themselves into the space and fell instantly asleep, both on their backs, Samaki's head on Mkono's chest. When he awoke, two hours later, Samaki's right ear felt remarkably pleasant; in his sleep Mkono's rubbery fingers were softly caressing it.

When next Samaki awoke, it was nearly dawn. He stiffened, forgetting for the moment the significance of the clawless otter scent that permeated the cavern and recognizing the absence of his mother's. Remembering the evening's romp, he relaxed. Then he stretched elaborately, nuzzled the sleeping clawless cub, arose, and left the chamber. Mkono never stirred; unused to wrestling in his solitary life, he had been taxed by so much activity and would sleep for at least an hour more.

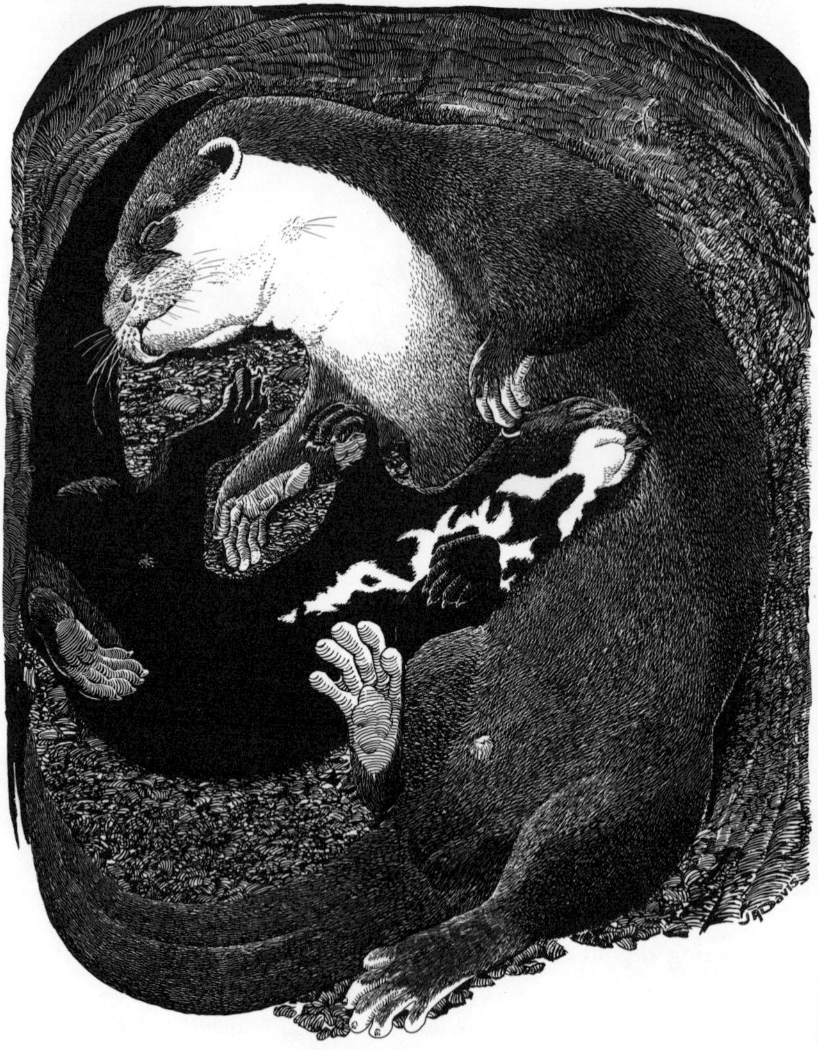

Samaki slipped noiselessly into the river to seek his breakfast. He had been little affected by the playing, so far as his muscles were concerned, but it did make him hungry. Having eaten, he set off upriver, where last he had seen his mother and her consort.

The adults weren't at the holt. Samaki scoured the ground for scent and found a track, but it ended at the river. Anxious, he piped his contact call, but no answer came. He slipped into the water and made his way upstream, stopping to check the bank and the rocks of the river for scent. On one sloping rock he found a fresh spraint bathed in urine that carried Maji's signature.

Sunlight had now spilled over the trees to the water. Minute bits of silt and organic debris scintillated before the cub when he moved below the surface; minnows glittered, passing from shadow to sunlit patches of the river, but Samaki had no time for them. Fulfilling his desire for the social comforts was not at all a matter of choice at this age, as it would be when he reached Mto's years—if he did.

When at last his calls were answered, in two voices, Samaki climbed the bank and raced toward his parents. The adults had just uncoupled, landed, and begun to dry themselves. They arose on hearing Samaki's chirps and met him, running as enthusiastically as he. The reunion was effusive, then boisterous. First the nuzzling, three noses probing fur almost feverishly; both adults were surprised at the lingering traces of Mkono's smell, but if it bothered them at all they showed no sign. They touched, nose to nose, nose to corner of mouth, to cheek, ear, shoulder, and flank. They poked under the base of Samaki's tail, half lifting his feet from the earth. Then the wrestling began, more intense than usual, because it had been half a day since the last time.

At length Mto withdrew from the game, and when Maji, too, tired of it, he turned to her with new attention—or rather with the same attention that had occupied him for the past few days. Maji felt his muzzle push under her tail, wedging toward her vulva. She wheeled around, lashing savagely at Mto's shoulder with open mouth. At her bite he pulled away and submitted to her harsh chittering. The time was not right. The big male ambled off downriver toward the den; Samaki followed, and Maji was not far behind. But while Samaki trailed the male into the holt, Maji found a shelter in a thicket and slept alone.

Late in the afternoon Mto arose. His stretching woke the cub, and the two moved above ground. To Mto's investigations Maji this time responded coquettishly; they slipped into the water again, and Samaki was once more at loose ends. He found himself swimming toward Mkono's territory.

The clawless otter was elsewhere, puddling a hundred yards up the small creek that emptied into the Mazingira. Frogs abounded here, and crabs, and invertebrates of many kinds, the latter to be had by turning over almost any stone. Mkono stopped his search every so often to filter any sound of danger that might be threaded in among the rush of the two small falls nearby, but he never detected Samaki's thin chirp. He disarmed a crab, held the struggling form in both hands, and crushed it, shell and all, between broad molars.

Samaki's search brought him around a finger of sand overgrown with weeds and left him staring into the cold, pale yellow eye of a crocodile floating some six feet away. This crocodile was half again as long as the one Samaki had vanquished yesterday, but yesterday's confidence urged the cub not to retreat, not just yet. Normally, a three-foot-

long crocodile confines its attentions to fish and small aquatic birds, but this one was still learning to gauge the size of his prey. He lay still, appraising the otter. He could see only the mammal's head, and its size was well within eating range. The armor-plated skull sank slowly below the surface. Samaki submerged, in turn, and the two enemies regarded each other, grimly silent and motionless. Fifteen seconds passed: The otter's period of comfortable submersion was ended. He could hold his breath for a considerable time more if he had to, but now it was an effort. Twenty-five seconds. Neither moved. Nearly a minute. The otter inched his head upward, but before he broke the surface the crocodile lurched forward.

Spent breath tore from Samaki's throat, wrenching with it a scream of terror. He wheeled in a shroud of spray. His kicks lifted him clear of the water to the shoulders, then he dipped and arched into a dive, but his tail, curving to follow the body, jerked taut, held near the tip in a vise of bone and teeth. At the brook Mkono heard the wailing scream, recognized it, and raced toward the river.

The reptile loosened his grip to snap again for better purchase, but Samaki whipped his tail away. The crocodile's jaws closed on water. He lunged again. The otter whipped his body to the right, but not quickly enough; two peglike teeth closed through the webbing of his left foot, one grazing the tissues of the fourth toe. The crocodile spun along the length of his frame like a dowel in a lathe, but instead of wrenching the otter's leg from its socket, the maneuver tore through the elastic web, and Samaki was free once more. He scrambled wildly up the gentle sand slope, but the saurian was close behind. Neither saw the clawless otter careen from the patch of weeds until he was astride the reptile, his mollusc-crushing jaws gouging through bony plate and fibrous tissue, fangs tearing their way to meet at the spinal cord. The crocodile thrashed and rolled over Mkono; the otter rolled them upright. Samaki by now had flung himself into the fight, stabbing at the thrashing tail, but it was too powerful to hold fast. He broke free and turned to the other end, where he savaged the throat. In his fury one of his bites closed on Mkono's forearm, causing the larger otter to interrupt his laborious destruction of the crocodile's neck. Seizing the opportunity, the reptile drove forward out of Mkono's clasp to the river. Both otters charged as far as the waterline, where they stood spluttering for a time, before each became aware of his wounds.

The crocodile made for deep water, where he plowed into the mud and lay still. The small cloud of silt he stirred up drifted downstream and settled to the bottom; a new substance discolored the water. Like smoke from a distant chimney, blood drifted, dispersing with the river's flow. The wounds were mortal.

CHAPTER 5

The cubs succumbed to a draining fatigue. They forwent the short walk to Mkono's holt, choosing instead to find shelter under a bush. Even so short a distance was hard to manage, once the excitement of the battle had died, for the clawless cub's arm throbbed from Samaki's bite, and Samaki's left foot hurt. Even such elastic membrane as his torn webbing was made of had sensory nerves within, and each step, each flexing of the web brought pain. It wasn't a great hurt, but enough; the injury to his toe hurt more. Samaki hobbled, then made his way on his three uninjured feet, adapting quickly to the new gait. Mkono had run on three legs before, one paw pressing a dead crab or an interesting shell to his chest, so his cripple's progress held no problem. Bedded down, each otter tended to his wound, licking it solicitously. When they slept their dreams were vivid and terrifying, and each woke the other with cries of alarm and fear.

Before the night had half passed the cubs awoke and, by some unspoken agreement, moved to the clawless otter's den, where sleep would be safer. The wounds ached, now worse than before, but each otter kept his injured limb off the ground, and the trip was bearable. Both slept through dawn. The sun was high before hunger drove Samaki to the river. In the water, three-legged progress wasn't too difficult, but more than a few fish escaped his lopsided thrusts. It was a matter of luck that he caught a catfish of good size; it had

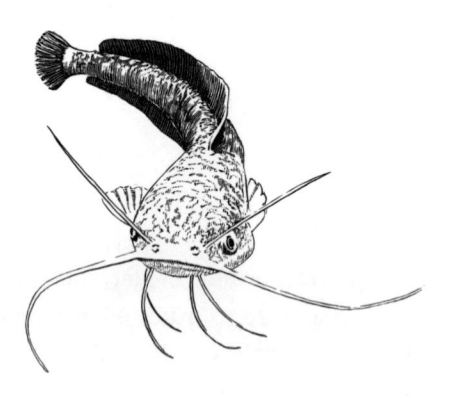

blundered into a cul-de-sac between two rocks, and there the young otter dispatched it. Ashore, he ate his fill, and there was enough left, still fresh enough, when Mkono hobbled out of the holt.

Samaki stayed another day with his companion before he felt able to travel. His foot would heal in short order, and once he made the necessary muscular compensations in swimming to offset the loss of part of the web, he would be as good as ever. The injured joint of the fourth toe would heal with a stiffening knob of tissue that would keep the toe permanently extended—its caw would grow longer than the others because of that—but within a week or two the spot-necked otter would, most of the time, be unaware of the deformity. The clawless otter would fare less well for a time, because grubbing with a single paw is terribly inefficient. Fortunately, an otter has a clean bite, and Mkono's gash had already begun to heal without infection.

When Samaki had not returned by the morning after his departure, Maji set out to search for him, and Mto followed. Their prolonged copulation of the afternoon before had been the last in seven days of concentrated passion. Four fertilized eggs floated free in the female's uterus, dividing and redividing, not yet ready to implant themselves in the uterine wall; that would take place in a few days.

Maji's scent no longer excited the old male, but her company still gave him pleasure, and now she was just an agreeable companion.

Samaki had just set out toward home when the two adults met him in a clearing. The old pattern of reunion played itself out again, and when it was ended, all three rested.

They met not far from Mkono's den, and not long after the three spot-necked otters had settled down to relax, the clawless otter awoke, stretched, groomed himself a little, and came above ground to find Samaki. He found three otters, two of whom got to their feet in postures of defensive alertness. The third sprang to his feet and dashed over. Samaki never tired of the near-ritual of greeting; noses burrowed into

[57]

plushy fur, poked and probed, and the small incisors of two species gently nibbled alien fur in a grooming protocol that is basic to the social mores of every species of otter in the world. Maji tensed, something in her urging her to defend her cub. Yet some other current of her mind inhibited the attack; it may have been, some would say, that her inborn maternal reactions were waning with Samaki's growth, but more likely the bitch recognized the absence of hostility in the encounter, perceived the common thread of affection in the grooming. She could never bring herself to approach the stranger in friendly greeting, nor could Mto, but her suspicion of this outlandish otter had lessened, and when she encountered him in the future she would see him in a slightly different light.

Samaki ran from Mkono to his parents, inviting the adults to romp, but they were unable to relax their vigilance enough to comply, and the clawless otter scent hung in his fur just enough to maintain their uneasiness. He scampered back to Mkono, but his friend, also, was now too uncomfortable to play. Samaki shuttled back and forth twice more, but the three otters, in spite of their common bond with him, could not coalesce into a single group. He was attracted to both camps, so nearly with equal strength that a confusion settled upon him. Midway between parents and comrade, he squatted abruptly to scratch frantically at an irresistible itch that had inexplicably arisen just behind his left ear. People, no less than otters, are affected by such itches at times of strong conflicting urges. It seems likely that nature has built in this common tendency toward inappropriate, but neutral, behavior in such situations to provide time for the mind to resolve its conflicts; at least the resolution often follows the dithering. When Samaki got to his feet again it was to trot back to the two adults with whom he had spent so much of his life.

≈≈≈

The otters played for a while, then sought out a sheltered place and slept. Samaki's sleep was a restless one; he awoke often, sometimes to an itch, sometimes to groom his fur, and sometimes merely to fidget. Once, he awoke to a peculiar sensation in his groin. His penis, buried beneath the abdominal skin, had swelled slightly, raising a ridge under the fur. The sensation was a pleasurable one, and the young otter responded to it as he did to anything new and interesting. He probed with his nose at the urethral orifice. A spot-necked otter has no external manifestation of his unerect penis except the opening of the urethra, his evolution's concession to streamlining. But as Samaki poked, the opening blossomed outward until the everted skin formed a disc about an inch in diameter, from which there protruded the tip of the penis, a quarter of an inch thick and some three times as long, like a flower's pistil. The otter, engrossed in this novelty, was supine, his torso curled forward. He grasped and pressed at the abdomen well to either side of the erect tissue and continued to nose at the apparition for long minutes, until, as otters do, he lost interest. The penis retracted, but remained partially turgid under the skin for perhaps a minute more. This reawakened his curiosity again, and the cub sniffed intently once more at the site of the disappearance, then licked the fur around it.

Somewhere overhead a small bird distracted him; he lifted his head high, curling his body into a dark crescent. The movement rolled his weight toward the hips, until he was resting solely on the base of his tail. He held in this seemingy difficult posture—an easy one for an otter, actually—for a long moment, and then, swinging his hindfeet to the ground, in one fluid movement he stood upright. But by this time the bird had long since gone; he trotted the few steps to where the adults still dozed. Samaki touched his mother's shoulder perfunctorily with his nose, glanced briefly at Mto, settled to the ground, rolled over on his side, and fell asleep again.

Some twenty miles down the Mazingira a female crocodile had been tending her brood of hatchlings, some fifty of them, for the past three days. Lying near the buried eggs, she had heard the hatchlings' chirping calls, muffled by several inches of earth baked hard by the sun. She had scraped away the earth and freed the baby crocodiles, then carried them to the water in her mouth.

On the Kilindi, Maji had become surly toward both her cub and Mto. She retired to her den and there gave birth to four cubs; fifty-eight days had passed since her mating.

The Long Rains, delayed this year, began. Afternoon skies lowered, ominous and sculpted of slate. Often the rains began in midafternoon and persisted, sometimes intermittently, well into the hours after dawn. At times the waters sluiced from the skies in dense sheets, and these rains disturbed Samaki. How strange it is that a creature whose life is so bound to water would find that element distasteful delivered in small packets. Mto was less disturbed by the downpours, but he, too, spent less of his day out of the den, and his activities, with Samaki following suit, now played themselves out more in the daylight hours between the rains.

The time with Mto was largely a time of play and a time for Samaki to sharpen his swimming and fish-catching skills. But there was a lesson or two to be learned from the older male as well. Once, as the cub followed his father to the shore, an insect's scuttling drew him away from the adult's wet track and off a few feet to the right. The beetle had just plunged down into a shallow depression, and when Samaki followed with his nose he drew a breath of pungent scent that overrode all further interest in the insect. For a long time he drank in the scent that pooled in the depression and in four lesser ones arranged at one end of the largest one. Mto looked back, and curious at the sight of the immobile cub, trotted over to investigate. One whiff of the musk in the depression and Mto leaped back with a sharp "Ffff!" Then he cast about, peering in all directions, still uttering the sound of his anxiety, and slipped into the river. Mto's alarm was contagious. Samaki, too, began to give the whispered cry and joined his father in the water. The cub knew now that the scent he had detected was something to be feared and avoided, but it is doubtful that he ever noticed with his eyes the outline of the leopard's pugmark.

Below the water surface the rains could be ignored, but they made themselves felt, all the same, in turbidity born of flood-washed mud that now cut visibility in the river. Fish could be found only at close range now, and the current, accelerated to deliver the stream's new burden, required new maneuvers by the otters.

The huge raindrops were the worst part of the season. On the rare occasions when one slammed into a whisker above Samaki's eye, his reflex blink was swift enough to keep the raindrop from hitting his cornea, but too many of the drops missed the whiskers. For the young otter the times of heavy rain were best spent in the den with Mto. When hunger made hunting necessary, he passed as much of the time as he could below the surface; but coming up for air still presented the hazard of inhaling raindrops, until he learned how to breathe safely—or rather, where. He came up for air one time close to the bank, under what was literally an umbrella of overhanging foliage. In the downpour tiny cascades ran from the leaves, but they were localized, and Samaki could keep his nostrils away from them. The tight, muscular valves that kept his nostrils closed and watertight while submerged were useless if they had to be opened for breathing; Samaki's discovery of the use to be made of foliage had been a chance one, but he required no further period of trial and error to add it to his repertoire. Mto, of course, had years earlier found the same solution to the problem, one of the many each otter must find for himself.

The rain fell in shapeless blobs, lumps of water almost, that struck like hurled projectiles before they splattered away. They plummeted to earth first in a loose scatter, then so fast and thick that it seemed as if there were more matter than air. They dashed the sandbars into a constantly shifting surface of little craters and bent leaf and branch into trembling submission. They bent the more slender grasses and fragile herbs and chewed the soil into bits small enough to be torn away and hurried down even the tiny slopes of minor depressions. They swept soil and pebble to the river, mixed them with the greater waters, and thrust all but the larger bodies onward with the swollen flow.

The long rains persisted through May and most of June. Life along the Mazingira went on, because it had to.

Birds went about their business, and butterflies, even, braved the heaviest downpours. Rodents in low-lying areas drowned in their burrows. Those that fled the waters were snapped up, most of them by predators in unfamiliar territory. Some of these the otters caught, but in general they spent little time out of the holt and played less. Only so much wrestling can be done in the confining vault of a den, and both Samaki and his father suffered small moods of irritation more characteristic of Maji than of their own personalities. There were bursts of bickering and an occasional intemperate bite, and by the end of the rains Samaki succumbed to the urge to wander off on his own. His leave-taking was as casual as so much that otters do. He left Mto devouring a small fish and simply swam downstream for a few hundred yards; then he hauled out and followed the bank at an unhurried pace.

In the first twenty-four hours he covered about a mile of the rivercourse, picking up interesting scents, hunting, and investigating sheltered hollows in the bank. He found a suitable temporary den before night came and slept through most of the dark hours, vaguely disquieted by the experience of being alone, all the more because in the den there lingered a faint trace of Mto's odor.

Late in the morning of the second day of his wandering, Samaki began to discern new otter scents—one that was also male and occasional patches of a strange female's musk. The latter interested him somewhat; the first was somehow unsettling, even without the knowledge that it was left by Mto's hostile neighbor. At first Samaki paused to sniff long and intently at each new scent marking, but the novelty wore off in time, and his rate of travel became less leisurely. He found a sheltered place before noon and slept away the afternoon hours. At dusk he was awake again, caught a labeo that assuaged his hunger, and continued downstream, sometimes on the bank and sometimes in the river. Late in the

evening he holed up again, this time in a hollow under a riverbank root, and he fell asleep with the air in the hollow permeated with the smell of the male he had yet to meet. It awoke in him a nervousness, but his need for sleep and shelter was greater, so he slept.

The twilight hours of predawn found the young otter abroad once more. He caught two small fish, one a young labeo, the other a fairly large minnow. The first he took to shore to consume, but the minnow he ate floating on his back, like a sea otter, holding the fish in his forepaws and crunching it loudly in his jaws. He dawdled awhile to swim merely for the exhilaration that loops and dives and sudden bursts of speed brought; the muscles and minds of other animals may find sufficient stimulation in the work of finding food, but otters are in a sense overdesigned for their work, almost too efficient at meeting their physical needs. Samaki's spirit demanded activity. If he could find his food easily—too easily, almost—then he must move himself through the waters, wrestle with a companion, wander, for the sake of these things alone. There was in him a joy in movement. The sensation of his limbs and torso moving as he willed was pleasure as great as any he knew. And the motions as often as not brought him new knowledge: how to move, how to turn more sharply or slow himself more abruptly, how to change his position in the water subtly but more effectively than before. Sometimes his play brought him face to face with creatures or things new to his experience, and his natural curiosity added new data about his world. So it was now; his sporting took him into sight of a turtle.

The turtle was hanging suspended from the surface, its head thrust into the air. It was the first such creature Samaki had seen, for upriver the current was stronger. Here the Mazingira widened, moved more sluggishly. At first the turtle was an object only, but an object to be investigated, warily, inevitably. Samaki surfaced quietly, recharged his lungs, and then sank again without a ripple into the brightening haze of the river. The turtle's legs moved lazily, correcting for a slow rotation of its body caused by the current. It was a living thing! The otter paused, sizing it up; not a crocodile, not a fish or frog. Although the shell might remind a human observer of a whirligig beetle, the similarity did not occur to Samaki—the difference in size alone was too great, and the movements of the two were not at all comparable. To the otter, form and movement are not separate categories to be pigeonholed, but an integrated complex of stimuli. No, this was something new, and it took Samaki little time to decide that it posed no danger. So, with only that small residue of caution that may spell survival, he moved toward the oval silhouette.

He was upon it; the turtle withdrew into its armored

fortress, leaving the otter to clasp in his forepaws an inanimate object. He hung on, doubling to hold the shell with his hindfeet as well, and slowly sank into the water with his booty. Halfway down Samaki released the shell and hung back to watch. Then, just as he was about to approach and grab it again, the shell sprouted a head, tail, and four scrabbling legs that sent it scuttling downward and away. Samaki spurted forward again in a shallow descent that took him under the turtle. He rolled over on his back as he did so, overtook the reptile, and came up a few inches ahead of it, eye looking into eye. The turtle, with the resignation of millennia, pulled in its head once more, flattened its tail against its soft thigh, and tucked its legs tight into the recesses between its upper and lower shells. It could wait. This turtle had met with young otters before and, safe in its hard case, would survive by the exercise of one of the few traits in which it far excelled any otter—patience. Samaki danced his graceful underwater dance with the inert turtle for a few minutes at a time; then, losing interest, he withdrew, and again the turtle came to life. On the third such reanimation, the otter understood the rules of the game, and thereafter he alternately captured his toy, withdrew, and allowed it a brief escape. Then he caught it again.

Even the best of games palls after a while, and in half an hour Samaki abandoned his unwilling partner, made for the shore, and fell asleep in a thicket. His dreams were of the turtle, and of his mother and Mto, and of a minnow he had been unable to catch earlier in the day. In his dream the minnow hung just out of reach, then darted out of sight only to reappear tantalizingly before him. In his sleep his legs kicked mightily, his body bending and straightening in the water of his mind. In midafternoon Samaki awoke, looked about and listened, and searched the air with his nostrils. Nothing was amiss; a malachite kingfisher called from a branch over the river, and a touraco from the forest on the other side. The otter slipped into unconsciousness again, but less deeply. Already his stomach hinted at hunger, but subtly, and it would be another hour at least before its hint would become a demand. He dreamed with his nose now, as a breeze from the river shifted. In his dream he was poking again at a weathered dropping, mostly bits of fishbone and scales bound with dried mucus and giving off the old scent of urine that carried the sign of the unknown male.

He was jarred from his dream by a loud snorting splutter in an unknown voice. And as he swung around to see the strange male, he heard the intruder's low growl, rising in pitch, more urgent. Samaki rolled to his feet. His movement prompted another splutter, followed by a savage rush. The young otter turned tail and raced for the river. The larger male was right behind him, spluttering. He followed Samaki into the water and pursued him for a distance before breaking off the chase. Within the hour the male appeared again, following Samaki's trail, and another attack took place.

Samaki was bewildered by the hostility he had been met with. Mto had never attacked him beyond an infrequent irritated nip, and his mother's recent irascibility had never been so prolonged or persistent. When next he came upon the hostile otter's spoor, a fresh mixture of stool and urine on a flat rock, he felt the thrill of fear and hastened away.

The fierce male's scent seemed to be everywhere, stale in some places, fresh in others. It had been no different in Mto's territory, but there the scent marks had borne a comforting message, one that Samaki had taken very much for granted. Here the scent carried a threat, and each new deposit put the young otter on edge.

For the next two days the antagonistic male pursued Samaki. From the resident's point of view, the young otter was an intruder—a competitor for food, resting places, and females. It is doubtful that the reasons for his hostility lay at all in the realm of conscious knowledge; it was a matter of survival for him. His territorial sense was more intense than Mto's, and his temperament generally more quarrelsome, but he was playing out a role that would contribute to his survival in the long run. Had Samaki remained with Mto much longer, his father's demeanor would have in time grown less cordial, at least within the confines of his territory—although it is true that, were Samaki to usurp the place of the hostile male, his meetings with Mto at their common boundary would likely remain friendly ones.

If the pursuit of Samaki was relentless, it was also sporadic, because the young otter left no trail of scent during the aquatic legs of his journey and did not confine his wandering to one bank of the river. Near the western end of the male's territory the Mazingira divided into two channels that embraced a large island, low-lying and overgrown with grasses that could survive the rain-swollen cycles of the river's existence. Part of the island was then awash, and Samaki found an abundance of invertebrates in the submerged vegetation as well as some small fish that were just settling into this newly habitable area, which they would soon be obliged to vacate as the river receded. He tarried only long enough to eat and then headed downstream once again.

June was about to relinquish the year to July when Samaki bedded down for the night. In his ears he had been hearing a different sound, a steady muffled roar that grew louder and threatened to drown out the river's usual murmuring. He was aware of the new tone, but it was distant and unconnected with anything in his memory. He slept fitfully, as he had since he had entered this alien territory, and he was up earlier than usual. Stars still twinkled in the river in the gaps of the mist, and only a stray bird or two was calling.

As the steady, distant thunder grew louder, the river pinched to a narrower, but deeper, bed between two precipitous slopes of rock. The waters picked up speed in their passage between the leaning walls, and the acceleration buoyed Samaki's spirits momentarily, until the realization struck him that he was no longer master of his movements. He was being swept ahead more quickly than he wanted to be, and when he turned toward the shore the sensation of being borne swiftly sideways disquieted him. He was swept against a rock, but he turned forward in time to absorb the impact with his forelimbs. Although the rock was submerged, he clung pressed against it until his need for air forced him to push sideways and away from his anchor. He set a course for the near bank, some twenty feet away, but beached some hundred yards below his target. Another hundred yards downstream the river plunged over the falls of the Mazingira.

CHAPTER 6

The falls of the Mazingira are among neither the broadest nor the highest in Africa. They span perhaps three hundred feet in five cataracts separated by spurs of rock, and drop no more than twenty-five feet, but they spill into a series of seething, rock-strewn pools with enough force to kill any otter swept over the edge. More than a few young otters setting out on their own had met their deaths here, and more than a few fish and crocodiles had filled their bellies downriver as a result of the waterfall's sporadic bounty. Samaki had been lucky.

He recovered quickly, as otters do, from the fright of being flotsam and, still curious, worked his way along the rocky bank to the place where the river disappeared into

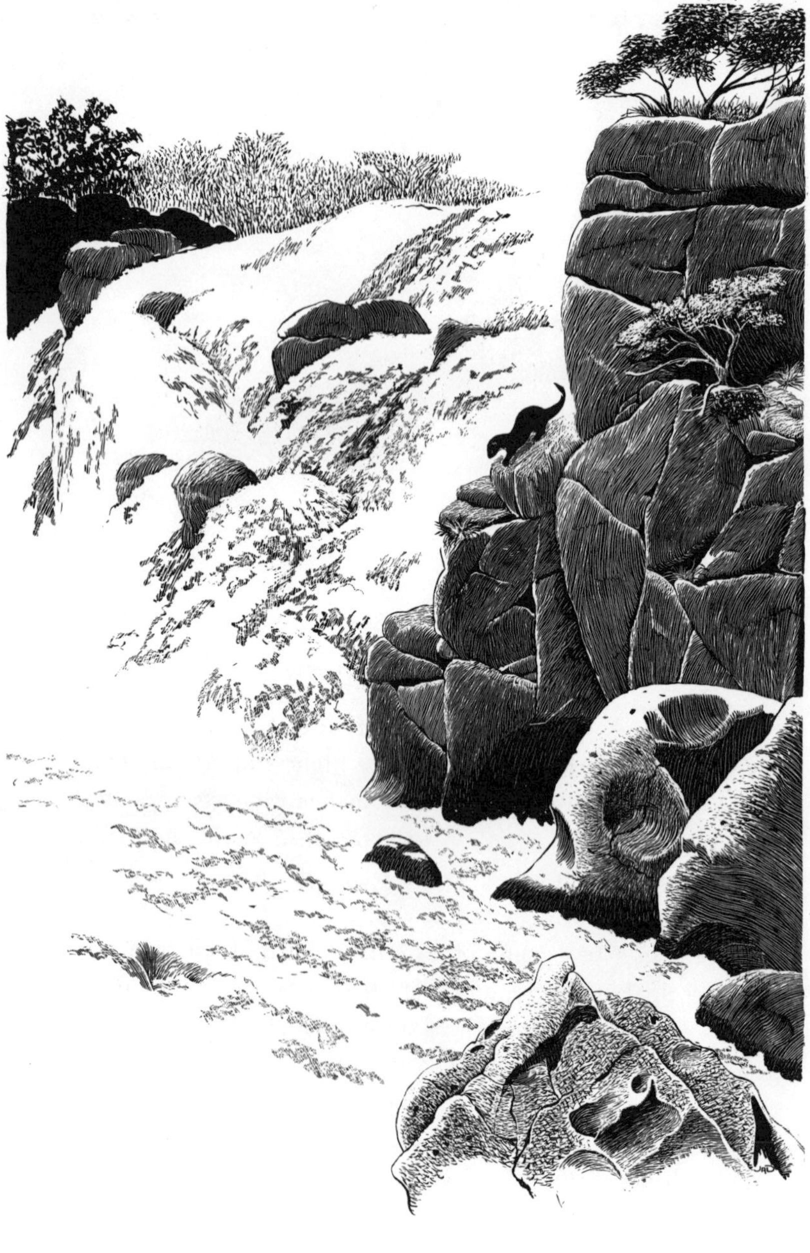

the air and steady thunder. Squatting pressed to a cap of rock, Samaki peered down a wall of stone cracked and etched like the skin of an elephant. At its foot the edges of the cracks were rounded by the waters, and the face of the rock had been smoothed and scooped out in shallow, soft-edged craters. Rocks, shorn of their hard edges, thrust out of the turbulent pools, glistening brown and wet on the faces turned toward the falls, dry and bleached gray where they faced downriver. Elsewhere the river's life lay chiefly in the creatures that held their commerce within it, but here, at the falls, the waters themselves were alive, and their writhing dance as they left the falls held Samaki fascinated. At length he reconnoitered and, finding a precarious route, descended toward the pools. It was a kind of vertical maze in which he had to retrace his path often. Small, scrubby shrubs, clinging tenaciously to what holds the rock afforded, more than once kept the otter from falling; his progress was accompanied from time to time by the dislodging of small chunks of stone, which would be ground smooth in the pools below. But he reached the bottom at last.

The descent took more than half an hour. When Samaki was only half the way down, the hostile male found his scent a few hundred yards above the falls. Still spoiling for another attack on the interloper, he tracked the youngster to the point at which he had taken again to the water, and here the male broke his pursuit. The falls marked the boundary between his territory and that of a male who lived below. The last few hundred yards of river above the falls were in fact a no-man's-land that this male had ceased to defend. He had long since learned to avoid the waters that could override his movements, and when the neighboring male had, on a few occasions, climbed the rocks, only to abandon the new area as an unsuitable foraging place, the hostile male had never been there.

The turbulence at the base of the falls was largely confined to the immediate vicinity. The southernmost cataract, down whose flank Samaki had traveled, plunged into a deep pool, then flowed swiftly, but smoothly, over a rim of rock to join the flows of the other cascades. Samaki detected another male's scent on the edge of the river, but he was too hungry to be much concerned. Below the falls were fish in abundance, fish that had claimed the area because of the small creatures that washed over the falls. The otter caught and ate several of the scavengers before he remembered the new scent.

He was wary now; when he came upon fresh droppings left by the occupant of this territory, he would sniff at them intently and leave the vicinity quickly. He had learned by now that traveling through the water was less likely to bring pursuit, so he spent less time on the bank whenever he encountered a scent mark. He covered half a mile of river before seeking a place to sleep. It was far later in the day than usual, and he slept well past sundown. He swam briefly, found a five-inch-long *Bagrus* catfish, and dined heartily. None of the resident male's scent markings were fresh here, so the young otter, more at ease, wandered up the bank into the forest that bordered the stream. The trail was physically a cleared line less than a foot wide, but it was also a ribbon of the overlaid smells of many animals. After only a few feet, he was startled momentarily by a mouse that scuttled across the trail almost under his nose. Reflexively, his head darted after the rodent, and his jaws came together through its spine. The taste was not at all bad, and he consumed everything but the tail. This was something new; he need not confine his hunting to the water alone.

Farther up, the trail's mélange of scents added a new odor—rank, fresh, and rodent. The last mouse had been a welcome change from the otter's usual aquatic fare, so he quickened his pace and followed the spoor until his ears registered an intermittent rustling in the leaf litter to his right. The sound halted abruptly. Samaki waited. After long minutes it began again, and the otter raced toward it.

No mouse kept its appointment with death, but a pouched rat. Eighteen inches long, with a white-tipped tail

of equal length, an elegant, sleek giant of a rat, he is an inoffensive distant relation of the rats that have taken over man's habitations. The rat had heard Samaki's approach, and it was waiting for him, reared up on its haunches, its forepaws clenched like a boxer's fists.

The sheer size of the rat took Samaki aback; he skidded to a stop, unsure what to do. Suddenly the rat seemed to swell. With a low, grating wheeze, it inflated both cheek pouches with air. As the otter stood rooted, the rat's face ballooned out, leaving only its muzzle and crown as they were. Wheezing steadily, the rat maintained pressure in its cheeks, and the sound added to its menace. Like many rodents, the pouched rat normally employs its expandable cheeks for carrying food back to its burrow, but it is the only species that has evolved a second, defensive use for the organ.

Curiosity began to overcome reticence; Samaki took a tentative step forward. The rat feinted in his direction, a short thrust of its upper body. Samaki could not be said to have run away, but his withdrawal was not a leisurely one.

Above him, the sounds of his scuffle with the rat set off a chorus of scattered barks reminiscent of the vervet monkeys near the place of his birth, but deeper and more ominous. The troop of olive baboons roosting above for the night had been disturbed, but settled down to silence again before the otter had gone far. He returned to the river, found a small tilapia, ate, and returned to his temporary holt, where he slept until sunrise; just before he awoke, the holder of the territory picked up his trail and followed it with some interest.

Mzee was an otter of uncommonly great age. For nearly eleven years he had held his own on the river; his teeth were no longer sharp, and while he could still catch large fish, he left the heavier bones uneaten. But he had survived longer by far than most otters. His knowledge of this stretch of river was great, and his wits had kept him alive. He was not an aggressive animal; twice he had been accosted over the years by younger would-be usurpers of his home, and each time he had retreated gracefully, avoided the newcomers, and bided his time for the month or two it took for fate to remove the less experienced challengers. In temperament he was much like Mto, and if anything, time

and age had made his good nature ever mellower. Mzee was thinner than he had been in his prime, and his muzzle was flecked with gray, but in all he was a handsome otter, with a mosaic of white and brown patches that ran from his chin to his chest and another mosaic that spilled over from his groin to the forward edge of his hindlegs below the knees.

The old one followed along Samaki's trail; not far away, he knew, was a shelter in a jumble of rock. In his mind's eyes he could see the broad, tilted slab that was its outer floor and the small-leafed woody stems that hung down in a spray to conceal most of the opening. Even more vividly he could smell the damp earth and leaf mold, hear the attenuated sounds of the river within, and feel the coolness and moisture in the air. Mzee knew where he was going, and he expected to find there a young otter male whose image in his mind was that of a complex pattern of scent. Not far from the rocks Mzee halted and settled down. He knew how simple the occupant would find defending this holt; he had done so himself. So he waited for the youngster to emerge into the open. To him the newcomer was a potential troublemaker, and this made Mzee wary, but not hostile.

Samaki opened his eyes, uncurled his body, stretched it as far as the walls allowed, and then relaxed all his muscles. He sniffed the air, listened to the muted sounds from outside, repeated the process, and crept to the opening with caution. He did not see the old otter at first, but when Mzee raised his head, Samaki froze. A slight breeze brought the adult's scent to him, confirming the otter's identity. The two stood silent for a moment until Samaki's ill ease brought a "Ffff!" from him. No growl answered, and no menace expressed itself in the old animal's demeanor; Samaki relaxed to a barely perceptible degree, and the other read the sign. Mzee had been aware, too, of Samaki's exhalation of anxiety; he saw that the younger male posed no threat, and he himself relaxed.

The younger otter advanced gingerly until he was no more than two feet from Mzee. The older one then stretched too, and when there were only inches between the two outthrust noses, Samaki performed a cub's gesture of submissiveness. Hindfeet firmly planted on the ground, he firmly twisted his head until it was cocked at a right angle to the ground. The motion traveled back along his body, neck and then chest twisting until he was half standing, half lying, shoulder to the earth and head nearly so. His mouth opened partially, and as Mzee made to sniff at his head Samaki pawed at the other with widespread fingers. The grizzled muzzle probed his cheek, his ear, shoulders, flank, and groin. When he had made his perusal, Mzee suffered himself to be investigated in turn and, satisfied, turned on his heel and trotted to the river. Something in his movement told Samaki that the old otter should not be followed. He set off on his own to feed his belly. The task took only a short time, and Samaki lolled awhile in the water, idly toying with a floating twig.

A sharp bark, like those he had heard in the trees the night before, drew his attention to the far shore, where the baboon troop was foraging. What had alarmed the baboons Samaki could not tell, but he knew that the sound was an alarm—it had caused a surge of adrenaline in his own bloodstream, as it had for the baboons, and beyond the trees five zebras stiffened to the alert, too. Whatever threat had prompted the alarm never appeared, and the animals slowly returned to their business. Samaki, safe in the river, relaxed first, although his interest in the large monkeys kept him at a high level of alertness. He treaded water for a while, then moved closer to the shore and treaded again only twenty feet from the low bank. The larger baboons regarded him briefly with a mild interest, but soon returned to the serious business of plucking tender grasses and snatching at such targets of opportunity as grasshoppers and an occasional small lizard. One small baboon left his mother to run toward the river's edge, fascinated by the dark head that hung offshore, just far enough away to allay any fear.

Like a little boy in his first long pants, the baboon had just replaced his scruffy black infant's fur with the sleek golden olive coat of adulthood, but the bare skin of his face was still the pinkish flesh color of childhood and would not turn dusky until the onset of adolescence. Samaki treaded water with stronger thrusts now, raising himself higher for a better view of the approaching baboon; this was too much for

the baby. He whirled around, screaming, and dashed toward his mother, who met him more than halfway and snatched him to her belly. The other baboons had stopped their activities at the baby's screams, and all eyes were trained on the otter. To the adults, an otter in these waters was a common sight; they returned to their business. But seven larger youngsters, who had been scuffling in a group, now watched Samaki closely. He sank until just his head was above water, and fourteen eyes remained on him. Clinging to his mother the youngest baboon craned his neck and peered at Samaki, too.

Samaki moved closer, but with caution, until he was a mere two yards from the bank and his feet grazed the river bed. He stood upright, and the septet panicked, barking. The dominant male, who had been watching the youngsters and the otter, turned to follow the fleeing juveniles with his eyes, but otherwise gave no sign of concern. His satellite males, all adults, looked nervously toward him and, reassured, relaxed again. One female, further from the river, clutched her black-coated infant at the barks, but the others seemed almost not to notice the uproar of the youngsters. Samaki watched for a minute, then lost interest and dove under the water.

When he surfaced a little downriver, two ashy brown waterbuck were eyeing him placidly. The character of the landscape was changing here; riverine forest was thinner than it had been upriver, and fingers of savannah reached to the water's edge. Zebras and gazelles, which elsewhere came to the river only to drink, grazed almost to the bank now, and too far away for Samaki to grasp their shapes, giraffes browsed dreamily in the canopies of acacia trees. The earthen banks of the river held the scents of many kinds of hoofs and paws and hands and feet, and each set within a species had a subtle signature all its own. The otter eased his way out of the water onto a sloping mud flat. The water rolled from his fur, and what still clung to the guard hairs held fast in tiny droplets, like crystal dandelion heads gone to seed. He shook as a wet dog does, but the motion, beginning at his forequarters, diminished before it had traveled far along his torso. Droplets flew from his neck and shoulders, leaving the guard hairs clumped into spikes that might have been ill-made reptilian scales. The spikes were smaller over his rib cage and almost nonexistent

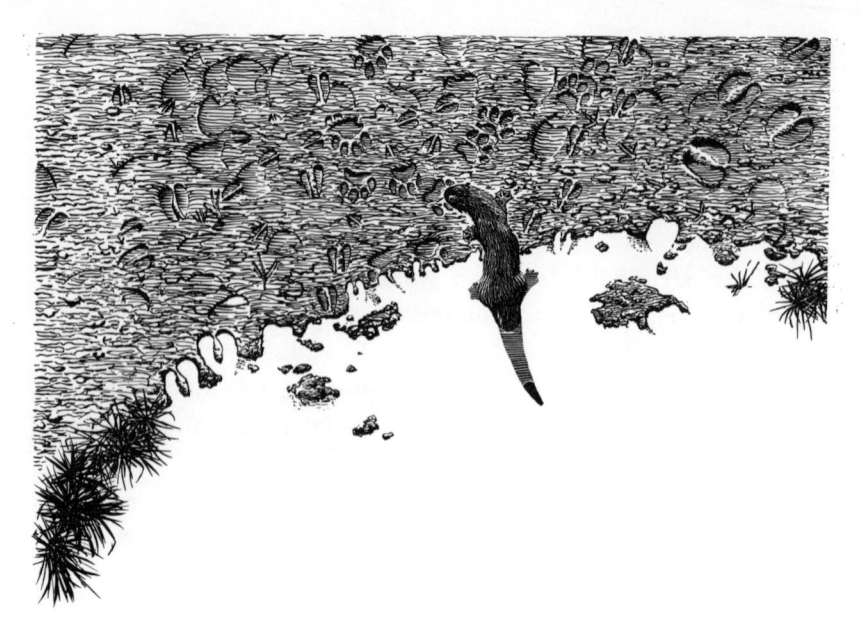

on his flanks, and the climbing sun was already shrinking the droplets that remained. Samaki's shake had been perfunctory; he was living at that moment through his nose, drawing in the riches of the overlapping marks of scores of feet. He drank deeply of one foot scent, then moved to another and another. So immersed was the young otter that he would have been easy prey for any large hunting beast, had one been nearby; but he was lucky. The lioness, into whose pugmark he was about to thrust his muzzle, had come to the river, lapped away her thirst, and left more than an hour ago. Then Samaki was there, breathing deep in her print. He drew back, going rigid and alert. There was no hint of transition: One instant he was a cub, reckless in his curiosity; the next, his demeanor was an adult's, all his senses acute, and his legs ready to catapult him away from the merest trace of a movement or a sound nearby or not so nearby. The scent-image of the leopard's pawprint not so many weeks ago and the echo of Mto's alarm scintillated in his mind and pushed an involuntary whisper of alarm from him. It was not the same smell, but it was the smell of something similar, close enough for him to recognize that it signaled danger. He peered about nervously, but the mud held almost no vegetation of size; the grass beyond was cropped short by scores of herbivores' teeth, and the nearest shrubs were far away. So the young otter sniffed more at the pugmark, adding its flavor to his memory. Then, the lesson over, he trotted back and melted into the river.

At first he surfaced at short intervals, turning to scan the river edge, the memory of his mentor's alarm at the cat scent replaying itself within him. But a minnow, flashing silver in the dappled light, put an end, for the time being, to further thought of the cat. If there are two universal characteristics of the minds of otters, they are short attention span and long memory.

Samaki's thought of the lion simply ceased to be, and in its place, as if it had always been there, was the darting image of the fish. And almost simultaneously, the otter was angling to the left, gaining speed, and closing the distance between himself and the minnow. Then the fish disappeared into a patch of waterweeds; Samaki plunged in after it, but could not find the fish. He cruised then, just above the vegetation, seeing no living things until his forward glide brought him over the edge of the patch. There, hovering a few inches above the river's bed, was a good-sized mudfish, still young, but a foot long. It hung below him, mottled khaki and gray body scarcely moving, except for small balancing movements of the pectoral and tail fins, its fleshy whiskers touching the bottom. The otter dove sharply almost as he saw the fish, closed the foot of water that lay between them, and bit into his prey just forward of its long, low dorsal fin. The fish thrashed, but Samaki subdued it with a series of bites and took it to the bank. He ate about half of it.

It had been a long morning. The young otter found a decaying log, its center rotted out. He clambered atop the log and rubbed his belly on it until the river's traces had been nearly all removed. He rolled over, wriggling in a sinuous and slow movement to dry his back, and then he repeated his rubbing on each side. Only then did he investigate the open end of the fallen trunk; finding nothing within to alarm him, he entered the sleep away the day.

With the lowering of the sun, a lion roared on the far bank of the Mazingira as Samaki awoke. He listened, but made no connection between the sound and the frightening odor of the pawprint of the morning. He arose, went to the river, caught two small fish, ate, and returned to the water again to sport.

Two days later Samaki was still within a half mile of the sleeping log. The large animals intrigued him, and the neutral reception he had received from Mzee, whom he had not encountered again, lent no haste to his travels. He was dawdling in the river as dusk blackened the shadows under a small water-edge copse of trees when two lionesses padded out from under the foliage to drink. Samaki treaded water and watched with fascination. Something, perhaps the way they walked, told him these were creatures of a different cut from the hoofed animals and baboons; something set him on edge. When the big cats had returned to the plain, the otter inched out of the water to where they had been and there found the rank cat smell hovering like an invisible fog in the depressions left by their feet. The scent awakened a memory, and in another part of his brain the sight of the cats flickered briefly again; a connection was made between the two and stored away. Now lions were no longer merely olfactory entities.

Samaki played again, this time with the conical shell of a snail, and when he tired of the game he sought out a cavity under a root in the bank and slept. That night he dreamed of the lions, and of his mother, and of the lions again, and of Mto's alarm at the leopard's pugmark.

CHAPTER 7

In the week that followed Samaki met Mzee along the riverbank trail once, but the old otter greeted him with considerable indifference and declined the young one's invitation to play. The scent of an adult female hung over some aging excrement on a rock, but Samaki had yet to meet her. He saw and studied the hoofprints of waterbuck, impala and gazelle, zebra and lion, and jackal. He began to wander more widely, but his travels centered on a usable holt, and he was no longer really pushing downriver away from his birthplace. Yet he was disquieted. Too many rocks and grass clumps bore traces of the old male otter, and once, on returning to his holt after an absence of two days, he found Mzee's signature within, strong and fresh. Something urged Samaki on, to seek, without knowing it, a stretch of river that held no other male's scent, a stretch of river he could make comfortable with his own markings. His own scent glands were changing the character of their secretions, making them stronger and male-scented as his maturing testes put higher levels of hormones into his blood. Under the influence of the male hormones, his baculum was growing from a mere sliver of bone in his penis to a longer, heavier bone with a defined shape, reminiscent of a baseball bat, heavy at the base and tapering toward the free end to thicken again slightly in a complex knob. His neck grew heavier by a small degree, although it would be at least another year before he reached his full development. But of chief import to Samaki, the odor of females was beginning to acquire a new and heightened interest, and his own smell would soon affect the interest of other otters in him.

That Samaki dawdled so long in this one area was due to Mzee's great age. The old otter's own male scent was waning, and he traveled far less widely in his patrols than he had in his prime. Yet his presence was there in the dabs of scent on his excrement, and these markers were telling Samaki that he was an intruder on another's land. As a cub he had found these scents interesting only, but, maturing now, he read new meanings into them. He was not yet old enough to be stirred to an attempt to drive off the old incumbent, but he had already come to know without need for reason that two male otters could not share a territory. So he moved on, to run the gauntlet of the male otters downriver, until he should find an unoccupied strip of water and land or unseat a resident.

Two miles downriver a tributary emptied into the

Mazingira, and the river widened. At the confluence of the two watercourses Samaki was surprised by the arrival of an adult female, who ambled up the bank as he was halfway through eating a large tilapia. Behind him he heard her whispered "Ffff!" and turned to look over his shoulder. She approached, head held stiffly out before her, warily, yet with the assurance of a resident animal. Samaki backed away a step or two as the bitch sniffed at the fish. It was a perfunctory investigation, and she turned in short order to face the young male again. He might have run off, but he didn't, and instead pressed himself to the earth while the female pressed her nose to the side of his face, gingerly at first, then firmly. He squinted the eye on that side and twisted his head to expose his chin and throat slightly. The female continued her examination, passing from his face to his shoulders, then to his flank, and finally, to his groin. Nothing in her movements carried a sign of hostility, so Samaki reciprocated her actions. The ceremony over, the female turned to the fish and consumed what remained with noisy gusto. Having eaten, she trotted to the river, voided her bowels and bladder on a rock, and slid into the water. Samaki followed, or began to, but the lure of her droppings was too great, and he stopped to smell them. Only after a long draft of the medley of the half-formed, half-viscous deposit did he raise again his head and, spotting the female out in the river, dive after her. Their play was vigorous, and the sun was high when, as if at a signal, they swam together to the bank and sprawled, asleep, in a thicket.

When Samaki awoke again late in the afternoon, the female was nowhere to be found. Her trail led to the river, only to end there. The young otter could not know that she had traveled diagonally across the river and up the tributary to her holt or that en route she had met the resident male and was otherwise occupied with him. The young otter's search for his companion transmuted itself abruptly into a search for food, as he became aware of his empty belly, and a small labeo accommodated that hunger nicely by blundering into a cul-de-sac between two boulders at the edge of a patch of waterweeds. Samaki ate it without leaving the water; then, remembering the female, he set off in the wrong direction, downriver, to seek some sign of her. Few rocks studded the river here, and Samaki investigated each one he found. On the first he smelled her mark, but it was old. He left feces and urine of his own and continued on. The next rock carried a more recent trace of the female, but it was tainted by a fresh overlay from the male who claimed this part of the river. Samaki left and continued downstream; a growing maturity and experience told him his welcome was over.

Late in the afternoon of the next day, another mile and a half downriver, Samaki was awakened in his denning place by a whiskered touch and the scent of another female, not so strong as the last female's, but somehow akin to it. At the unexpected touch, he whipped his head around almost by reflex, his jaws slashing. Because he had lashed out from the sharp brink of sleep, his aim was poor, and he only grazed the cheek of the intruder. She flattened herself submissively and lay still.

Nadra was six weeks younger than Samaki. She and her sister had only a day before set off on their own; they had scrambled up the bank that night to blunder into a prowling python. The sister had come nearer to the snake, and the snake had suffered several deep rents in its slick hide from her teeth before she suffocated within the iridescent knot of its massive coils. Nadra had rushed in and bitten, too, but whatever harm either otter's slashing did would not affect the snake for some days. The sister died quickly, and when the reptile turned its unblinking eyes on Nadra she fled in panic, spluttering without control until she was far away from the lurid feast.

Nadra was a strangely colored otter, light milk chocolate, like a giant rat, but the dappled pattern of her throat was that of a spot-necked otter. The unusual lightness of her coloring, if Samaki noticed it at all, was of no interest to him; she had the shape of an otter and, more significant, the smell of one—a musk that was to his adolescent mind more fascinating than any he had inhaled before. He touched his nose to her muzzle, then worked his way backward until he reached her groin, where the focus of the exciting new scent lay. Burrowing his muzzle under her body at the base of the tail, he drew in deep drafts of the musk, lifting her hindquarters off the ground in his eagerness. Nadra responded not at all, submitting inertly to the investigation that as yet had no special meaning for her. When Samaki had done with his inspection and made no

hostile move or sound, the young bitch, in turn, studied the scents of his pelt, except that she lacked his preoccupation with the sexual odor and left his underside unprobed. Satisfied, she left the den, followed by the young male, and ambled toward the river, glancing back over her shoulder from time to time to assure herself that she was being followed. There was a subtle, twisting toss of her head as she ran, a coquettish gesture that was probably more an expression of her desire to play than a real signal of invitation. But Samaki was close behind her, and the two slid into the water as if they were the undulating parts of a single being. A water beetle scuttled downward, aslant, away from Nadra's whiskered approach; normally she would have chased it, but now she had a companion of her own species again, and she had no time for beetles. Samaki saw the beetle too. He felt the exultation of the rollicking about to begin, but the beetle was irresistible. He swerved slightly to his left and below, scooping the insect in his left forepaw and pressing it to his chest, all without noticeably affecting his pursuit of the female, and then he was abreast of her, hanging at the surface, the two of them breathing the river air. Nadra eased into a lazy dive; Samaki pushed over and reached out to clasp her torso, oblivious now of the beetle clawing its frenzied way to the safety of the river bed. It sped into the haven of a mat of algae there, while far above the two otters rolled and looped, their cadence now stately, now a wild saraband. Samaki had forgotten the faintly arousing scent of the other's femaleness. She was simply another otter, companion against loneliness, and it was enough.

For five days Samaki and Nadra frolicked in the river, caught fish together, though not in a cooperative manner, investigated the shoreline together, and denned together. They remained largely within a restricted area, Samaki hesitating to push very far down the river because of the presence of strong male scent markings in that direction. The young female felt no such inhibition at the scented places, and, still seeking a new home, she left Samaki toward the end of July. He followed for a small distance, but the presence of the resident male damped his enthusiasm. On the last day of July the incumbent male ceased to be an olfactory presence only. Following a courtship lower on the Mazingira, he had begun again to patrol his realm, and he found Samaki sprawled lazily on a broad slab of rock some distance from the bank. The younger otter was not quite asleep, yet he was drowsy enough not to have been aware of the second otter's approach. The latter hauled up noisily on the table of stone, head lowered, and growling. The sound was low in pitch and volume—a moan, almost—but when Samaki leaped to his feet in surprise, the swift movement pushed the other's growl higher in pitch and loudness. It resembled a moan no longer, but had a sharp edge, a mounting flavor of fury and a roughness it had not had before. Without preamble, Samaki launched himself into the river and streaked for the far shore. His pursuer followed him nearly to the shore, but the haste of Samaki's departure seemed to satisfy the older animal, and he broke the chase. Later he would scour both banks until he drove the intruder from his boundaries. The resident toyed with a stone for a while, caught and ate two tilapias, and took a

half-hearted nip at the dangling feet of an Egyptian goose, but always his memory brought forth the image of the trespassing newcomer, and always he lost the train of his interest of the moment to assure himself that he was alone on his piece of the river.

Eight days passed. Samaki was well clear of his antagonist's territory, and he had not yet come upon any sign of another male, other than traces so weak he could not be certain they were there. But he did find evidence that Nadra had been past, and on the sixth day he began to find excreta of an adult female. In the next few days he covered three and a half miles of river before he found the markings of another male. He had found an unoccupied territory, vacated through the agency of an enormous crocodile that had cruised eastward, up the river, on a temporary excursion from its own precinct. Samaki began to settle in; he lost the wary expectation of being chased off, and his own scent markers accrued steadily on exposed rocks and roots, adding to his confidence. The second time he met the downriver male he did not flee, but stood his ground, reading correctly the other's less than assured threats. But this stretch of the Mazingira was not quite like any of its parts that Samaki had known. He still had many things to learn.

CHAPTER 8

The Mazingira was wider here. Its flow gentled considerably, and the character of its aquatic inhabitants was somewhat unlike that of the upper reaches to the east. Dense beds of reeds grew along parts of the north bank, and the bank itself was low and sloping. The south bank, where the river turned slightly northward, was steeper, cut by the current, and the water exposed the roots of trees and wore hollows beneath them. Here and there the river's relentless chafing undercut a tree, leaving a cylindrical gangway on which turtles basked and waterbirds perched on stalked legs. A plexus of roots anchored the fallen trunk firmly in the earth, for a while at least. Its surface portion formed a maze of passageways for small

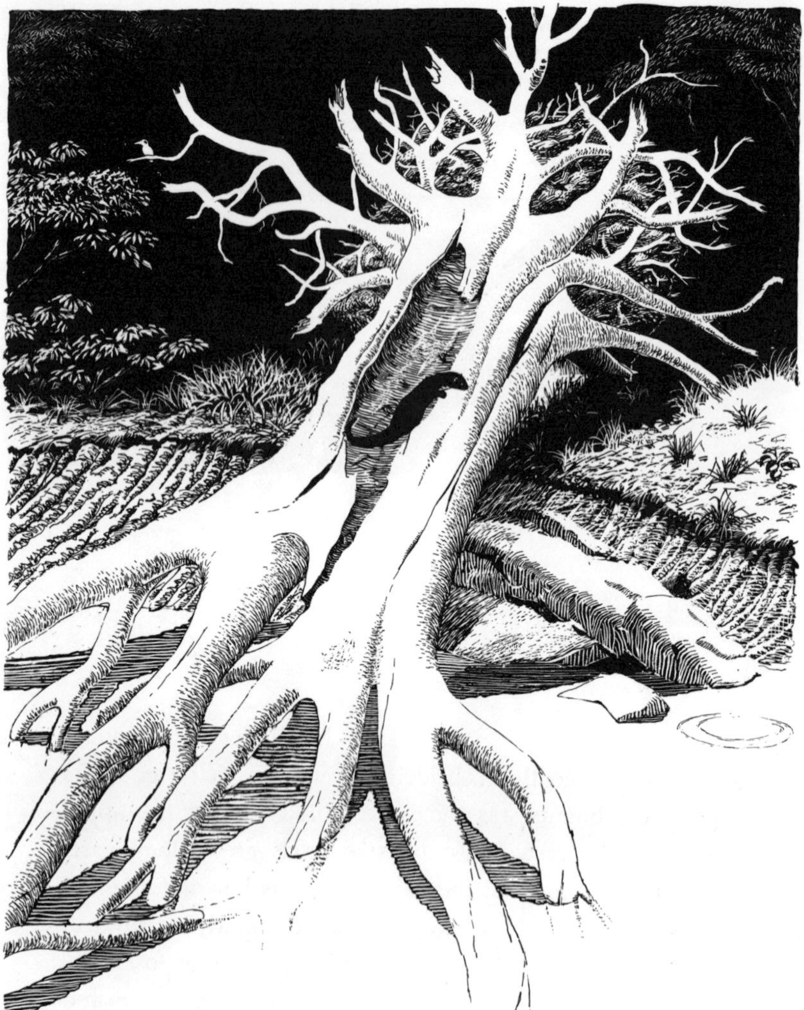

creatures, and the upthrust fingers of twisting wood made resting places for small birds and dragonflies. Under the river, decaying branches and twigs and twiglets wove a permeable net in which many lesser fish and invertebrates found comparative safety. For Samaki these trunks were ideal hauling-out places, their weathered surfaces absorbent and perfect for rubbing his fur dry. One huge bole in particular, long the ghost of a tree by the time it fell, had been cleaved in life by a thunderbolt and split. The elements had smoothed and worked the split wood, with the aid of countless insects and a passage of time. The tree had fallen with its wound uppermost to the sky, and long years of rains and mold and insects had reduced the inner surface to fragments and swept them away, leaving the massive trunk concave. With further rot the wood had become spongy, and generations of otters had worn it further, their rubbing, sometimes languorous, sometimes animated, abrading the core with velvety rasping. This tree was Samaki's favorite, a guardpost from which he could survey his river from over elevated ramparts, unseen by any creature not at home in the air. From just above the water he could watch for fish below, and in the punky hollow of the ancient column he could dry his fur with an ease he had never known before. Long ages past, in otter terms, swallows had excavated a nesting tunnel among the lower roots, and some long-dead otter had expropriated and clawed the bore wide enough to provide shelter. The holt suited the young otter so well that he adopted it as his principal residence, and although he found half a dozen other denning places, some better in many ways, the big tree was the one he used most consistently.

The tangle of what was once the tree's top, where the branches and twigs had so long ago pierced the waterweeds and mud of the Mazingira's bed, was the daytime retreat of a fish as strange in its way of life as it was in appearance. Normally Samaki would not hunt at the very doorstep of his den, but he returned from his first evening foray with less than a full belly, and he was still searching, as a matter of course, for something to eat. In the underwater gloom the elephant-trunk fish's bronze skin looked darker than by day. Its long slanting snout gave it the appearance of looking downward at an angle from its body, and a long, dark dorsal fin tapered, standing like the mane of a pony, almost to the forked tailfin. Its movements, though rapid at times, seemed stiff, without the sinuous grace of other fish, and it moved in the tenuous envelope of a very weak electrical field. Like the other members of the family Mormyridae, it navigated by detecting the changes in the field made by objects deflecting the flow. The field itself originated in modified muscles of the narrow tail stalk, a change of function that may account in part for the stiffness of the elephant-trunk fish's movements. But in part, too, its movements were governed by the need to avoid disrupting its electrical field. Yet its lack of strong lateral motion was no handicap; it could swim backward as well as forward and could move swiftly enough to capture the aquatic larvae of small chironomid flies. Its eyes were small and covered with skin, their function of secondary importance to the specialized electrical sense.

The elephant-trunk fish was alone. Strongly territorial, it had long since staked out its patch of weedy river bed in the tangle of branches and defended that area from all others of its own species. There it found an ample supply of larvae on which to grow; it measured eleven inches, with the potential to reach nearly three times such a size. But its potential was never to be realized.

Samaki cruised slowly just beneath the surface, sculling slowly and infrequently with his hindfeet. The water, turbid by day, was a vast shadow by night in which only an occasional silvery glint disclosed a swimming fish. Samaki had been unsuccessful since he began his search, so he changed his tactics. He dove into the bottom weed bed and began an unhurried, but not at all stealthy incursion in hope of surprising a frog or coming upon a snail. The elephant-trunk fish, foraging just outside the submerged crown of the tree, sensed a disruption of its electric envelope. Nerve endings deep in jelly-filled pits in its head sent impulses racing to a brain extraordinarily large for a fish. The intrusion was somewhere in front of the fish, so it backed quickly away and in so doing brushed against the weeds behind it. Samaki noticed the movement, spurted forward, and nearly had his prey. The fish darted backward again, and only the otter's whiskers made contact. But it was enough. More quickly than it takes to tell, Samaki's head shot forward and to the side, and his jaws closed on the fish.

On the tree trunk Samaki ate the fish. Its mucoid coat did not bother him, but when he bit into the meat of the tail a mild tingle, not at all strong enough to be painful, but disquieting in its strangeness, caused him to drop the last of his meal and paw it warily. His next foray brought him a frog.

The comforting presence of surroundings that were growing familiar worked a change in Samaki. In his early months, even when his world flaunted novelty before him by the hour, he had known an unconscious confidence born of a recognition of landmarks and bolstered by the almost constant nearness of his mother and Mto; the months of his independent wandering had kept him in an aura of wariness and an unidentifiable discontent, when every rock and tree stump belonged to another who might claim his right of ownership at any moment. Now Samaki had a home again, one which was not simply there, as in his infancy, but which in some way he understood he owned.

On his first excursion to the western limit of his range, that is to say, to the point at which another male showed resentment at his approach, Samaki met his first hippopotamus. He met six of them, in fact. It was late in the morning. Samaki had dined at dawn, poked about in the stream for a while, rested briefly on a gray block of stone, swum to shore, and then dawdled his way along the south bank in the direction of the current. He was in no hurry; he had to investigate every feature of his new home. When at last he slid into the river, he made for the north bank and its reed beds filled with small fish and water insects.

As he emerged from the reeds Samaki spied a large, gray boulder just higher than the water level. A lily-trotter stalked with pompous strides along its top, stopping now and then to pluck something from the surface. It was a fine hauling-out place, and it had for the moment the added attraction of a bird to chase squawking over the water. Because he had no serious designs on the bird, Samaki swam at the surface, slowly enough to avoid alarming the lily-trotter; six feet from the edge of the rock the otter sped forward and burst out of the water. Even as he scrambled up, he was aware of the softness of the rock and simultaneously of its unexpected smell. Before his attention could be pulled by these sensations away from the wild flight of the bird, the rock lurched, and a cavernous mouth, set in a huge, lumpy head, flashed from the water and swung toward him. Samaki leaped backward, striking the water with a graceless whack, and churned away at maximum speed. When his courage returned and bolstered his curiosity, the young otter sank deep into the water and approached the bulky form slowly and warily, ready for instant flight. Seen broadside below the water, the hippo was clearly an animal, and beyond him were the dimmer forms of five others. Days later, when next Samaki was in the vicinity, he came closer to the big beasts and soon discovered that they were tolerant of his presence so long as he came no closer than a few feet from them. A hippo's head, seen from just above the surface, had protruding nostrils and eyes and small, mobile ears that twitched wildly when the head broke the surface and were terribly difficult for a young otter to ignore. Samaki hungered to pounce upon these gyrating appendages, to wrestle with such lively entities, but he remembered the slashing, gaping maw beneath them and exercised a restraint rare in an otter.

There was something else the otter found fascinating about the hippos; each one was attended by a cortege of carp-like labeos nibbling delicately at its hide. Hanging there, lost in concentration, at their work, these grazers of the algae on the hippos seemed like easy prey. Samaki studied them long and intently, interrupting his observations only long enough to replenish the air in his lungs. By now he was hesitant about swimming too near the hippos, but the prospect of an easy catch eventually overwhelmed his good sense, and in time he made his move. Drifting slowly nearer a hippo, he chose his target: an eight-inch-long fish, gray blue like the hippo on which it nibbled. Samaki hung motionless for a time; then with sudden force kicked backward his webbed feet and darted in. He had the fish in his jaws, pushed himself backward from the behemoth with both forepaws. It was a mistake; the hippo, accustomed to the delicate touch of the fish, reacted violently. The boulder of flesh jerked upward, heaving water up and away in a fearsome splash, then plummeted back under the surface in a storm of streaming air that broke into bubbles and rose again. Samaki heard the turmoil, rather than saw it, for he was by this time far from the site of the disturbance. On the bank he ate his booty, the last fish he would snatch from a hippo's protection.

∽∽

There were in this part of the Mazingira a number of very young crocodiles a foot or so in length, the hatchlings of the large female and larger male that lived a few miles below. These juveniles Samaki dispatched when he came upon them; they were an enjoyable addition to his menu. The otter was only one of a wide diversity of vertebrates to thin the ranks of each year's batch of crocodiles. Storks and cranes of several species lanced them from the water; large fish burst upward to pluck them from the surface; mammalian carnivores, from the smallest mongooses to the leopard, found them targets of opportunity on the banks; even larger members of their own species preyed upon them, and the few that survived to reach a commercially acceptable size would have also to contend with human predators.

The small crocodiles were easy enough prey once Samaki devised his killing strategy. His two earlier experiences with the reptiles were still with him, and he was at first chary of the individuals that measured nearer two feet than one. But after a pricking bite from a small crocodile he had seized amidships, he went thereafter only for the neck and the back of the head and soon abandoned head bites because of the massive bone of the skull. Taken by the neck, a crocodile of small size could be easily decapitated; with practice, Samaki found the larger ones almost equally vulnerable.

Within his own part of the river, Samaki never encountered a crocodile more than two feet long. Further downriver were a few of the saurians that measured five feet or more, but only one pair of truly large beasts, a male sixteen feet long and a female nine feet. Growing crocodiles between two and five feet long are scarce, or at least they appear to be. Certainly there are not many of such size, for the rate of attrition of young crocodiles is almost unbelievably high. Still fewer attain greater size, but these are by their very magnitude most conspicuous, and because they are, their ranks are further thinned by humans.

The hippos never came upriver from the western end of Samaki's territory, but the otter made it a point to patrol that region more frequently than he might otherwise have done. The hippos fascinated him beyond any other nonprey species he had yet encountered. It may have been their enormous bulk and the dreamlike way they moved—they could be said to gambol at times in the buoyant murk of the river—or their generally inoffensive nature. Left alone, the hippos showed little interest in the otter, and he came to apprehend this in short order. There is no doubt that he was also attracted to the hippos by the numbers of fish that attended them, and the hunting in their vicinity was good so long as it was directed at the fish at the periphery of the behemoths' court. But the gray giants were themselves too fascinating to ignore for long. As weeks passed Samaki grew familiar with them, learned to gauge their movements under the water and to give them a wide berth when he encountered them on their nightly grazing forays on the banks of the river; at such times they tended to be less tolerant.

By day the hippos lazed in the river or slept on the flats, their backs exuding an oily, rust-colored ooze. They wore clear paths from the river to their nocturnal grazing places, and these paths were used by other species, large and small, bound for the river to drink. Samaki, too, made occasional use of the hippo trails on his investigations of the inland terrain, but much of the time he preferred to use the pathways made by lesser creatures whose eliminative habits were more tidy than the hippos'. Here and there along the hippo trails were what appeared to be the results of explosions of manure; the grasses and branches of shrubs were festooned with fetid shreds of chopped, partly digested grass stems. The hippos have adapted their eliminative behavior to serve the added function of territorial marking. But rather than merely dropping their loose, weedy stool, they broadcast it with a wildly whipping tail, and the result is an area that demands a wide detour.

Samaki had followed one such trail some fifty yards away from the river on a search for a tasty species of beetle that had emerged the day before in some numbers. He found a dozen or so quickly enough, poked about the earthen fortress of a termite colony, and then sought out a familiar tree, with a deep hollow, in which he intended to sleep away the remainder of the morning.

He was brought awake by a raucous chorus of banded mongooses foraging through the grasses and under shrubs, flipping over bits of fallen bark and small stones, each mongoose announcing its whereabouts intermittently to the others. Unlike mongooses of a more typical cut, these were comparatively stocky, short-tailed animals, their brownish coats decked out in narrow vertical stripes of darker brown from shoulder to rump. One, rummaging near the tree in which he rested, attracted Samaki's attention, and he rolled forward to peer out of the hollow. The mongoose flipped a chunk of bark over as Samaki's head emerged. Under the bark lay a millipede, shiny black and about as long and broad as a man's thumb. Unlike most millipede species, it had a flattened body, not a high cylindrical one, and it lacked the double battery of glands that ooze a volatile noxious chemical that is the defense of those lowly, slow-moving creatures. This millipede had a different defense; it rolled up immediately into a tight ball about the size of a filbert nut and as impregnable in its hard shell. The mongoose took his prey into his mouth and bit down on the sphere. His teeth slid harmlessly off the millipede's glossy shell, but the attempted bite was a perfunctory one; the mongoose had not really expected to be successful. Immediately he took the arthropod between his forepaws, jockeyed his position until he was facing away from the tree trunk, and then, in an almost simultaneous suite of movements, hopped upward with his hindlegs and hurled the millipede backward between those legs. The mongoose's prey smacked against the

tree and ricocheted off. When the little predator retrieved his missile, one of its armored segments was cracked, and his canine tooth drove into the fracture. He tore the creature apart and ate all but a few scraps that fell to the ground.

Then he scampered off to rejoin his troop, unaware that he had been observed by the otter.

Samaki left his shelter to investigate the fragments the mongoose had left. He recognized the scent of the mongoose as one he had encountered on trails before, but he had little time to dwell on that; the scraps of chitinous shell and tissue were inviting. He sniffed at them; then, very gingerly, took a small piece in his mouth. The taste was agreeable, and he took the remaining pieces, barely enough for a taste. Something of the experience filed itself away in his memory.

On his return to the river Samaki found a fresh deposit of urine and feces on the bank; it carried the signature of a female, one he had found other traces of before, but had

not yet met. And a few yards farther along the bank lay an otter, sensuously rubbing its back on a shelf of rock.

Samaki advanced slowly, head stretched stiffly forward. The newcomer rolled over and raised its head. A breeze arose on the river and carried the stranger's scent toward Samaki, the same he had just found on the bank. It was not

[112]

another male. Samaki relaxed somewhat. He stepped forward again, more confidently now. The female had remained where she was, nervous and alert, yet ready to assert her territorial right should Samaki prove to be a female. They were almost nose to nose before she recognized him as a male. She chittered, shrill and staccato, in his face. Samaki held his ground; then, his whiskers fanned forward, he moved his muzzle up to the female's, meshing the bristles.

Chumvi was three years old. Her throat and chest bore less a pattern of spots and blotches than a sprinkling of

white flecks, as if they had been liberally seasoned with salt. Her groin was flecked in a like manner. The year before she had borne a litter of two cubs. One had died in infancy of a fever, and the other had set off two months earlier downriver, where the old crocodile awaited him. Samaki's domain had then still been tenanted by the adult male otter, but he had more recently followed his son into the reptile's maw.

The two otters stood, whiskers interlaced, each drawing air laden with molecules of musk into flared nostrils. Samaki withdrew first to continue the ritual of investigation, and when he was done he submitted to a reciprocal going-over. Since Chumvi was not in heat, Samaki treated her as a companion only, but traces of something in her urine and on her person awoke the seeds of a different kind of interest within him. He thrust his nose under her hindquarters far more now than he had ever done with another otter before, and at times partial erections caused his penis to stand in bas-relief against his abdominal skin, like a mole's tunnel on a lawn. His baculum, the long bone that lay buried in his penis, was no longer an undifferentiated sliver, but had lengthened and was beginning to take on its adult form. Had Chumvi been in a state of sexual readiness, Samaki's own latent sexuality might have been awakened, but he was still an adolescent, innocent of any compulsion to mate, and his time was not yet. The two sported in the waters of the Mazingira, separated, and met again in the evening, to enjoy each other's company again. Chumvi left him when the night was old, to return to her holt, and Samaki made his way back to the holt in the bank, within the roots of his tree. Just as he reached his den a light rain roughened the river.

It was the first rain of the season, three weeks earlier than usual, and just enough to moisten the ground and bring out myriad small invertebrates. It had fallen in the late hours of evening, and the morning came clear and bright. Samaki had fished and dozed, and now as the sun climbed he made his way through a small copse of trees in search of insects. As he passed a large trunk, a movement attracted him—the slow flowing of a glomerid millipede. Anything that moved was a potential morsel or at least a plaything. So he poked at it with his paw and raked it to the ground, where, by the time it landed, it had rolled into a ball. He batted it off to one side with a spread paw, then dashed after it to push it several feet with his nose. Then he batted it again, retrieved it in his mouth, and tossed it, with a flick of his head, over his shoulder. He pounced upon it, held it between his paws, fell onto his back, and rolled it against his chest. Something about the smell of the hard sphere and its texture awakened a memory, which flowered into a vivid phantom of taste. The taste of the scraps left by the mongoose. Without further delay Samaki engulfed the ball of

flesh and chitin in his broad mouth, maneuvered it with his tongue toward one carnassial tooth, and drove his jaws together. The millipede had come to rest against his thick cheek, which anchored it enough to keep it between the opposing teeth. The blade of the carnassial cracked the armor and cleft the millipede neatly, and in no time at all Samaki chewed it, with loud crunching sounds, into a mass of meat and finely comminuted shell, all of which he swallowed with elevated chin. He searched then for other millipedes, but found none and returned, without disappointment, to the river.

For a month Chumvi was a frequent companion, but the relationship remained a casual one. Except for dozing together occasionally on a rock or under an overhanging bush, the otters denned separately. The rains meanwhile began to fall in earnest and continued into the first week of December. During the rains of May and June, Samaki had learned to use sheltering growths of foliage in downpours and to adjust his schedule of activity to avoid the most likely times of rain, so the season affected him minimally. He did spend more time than usual in his holt, and the increasing suspension of silt in the swelling river was a nuisance, but he took these changes in stride. The rains were an added bother in that they dashed away his spraints, his declaration of ownership of the territory, and when he noticed this he was compelled to travel more widely as the weather allowed. The showers washed away Chumvi's spraints as well, and this meant fewer opportunities for either animal to trace the other's whereabouts. Their meetings became fewer while the wet season held sway.

CHAPTER 9

The adjacent male's territory downriver, which began where the hippos bathed, was an unlucky stretch of river. Its ownership among otters had changed frequently because of the presence within it of the two large crocodiles and some lesser ones. Matata, a two-year-old male spot-neck possessed of an exceptionally aggressive disposition, had moved in in August, shortly after the previous incumbent had perished. Matata was not a particularly bright otter, and he had in the months just past had two close calls, once with the huge old male crocodile and once with the big female. He had avoided the reptiles as much as he could, but they had a way of appearing without warning at times, and after a third narrow escape a week

[117]

after the end of the rains, the otter moved eastward, upriver. He had met and put Samaki to flight on several occasions at their common border, and now he would move upstream, dispossess his neighbor, and take possession of a safer piece of the Mazingira.

Two days after Samaki first came upon Matata's scent markings well within his own boundaries, he found himself face to face with the invader. They met on a trail that followed the south bank of the stream. Only a few yards separated them when they became aware of each other. Both otters halted abruptly.

"Fff!" Samaki gave whispered voice to his anxiety. Again, "Fff!" He was edgy, and yet he was not frightened— or not very frightened. The other growled, and in response a growl crawled from Samaki's throat. Matata's low snarl rose higher, growing louder, working its way toward becoming a scream, and by the time it was indeed a scream

he was hurtling toward Samaki. He fell upon the younger otter, clasping him in his forelimbs, but Samaki had reared to meet the onslaught, and he, too, clutched the attacker.

Matata bit savagely at Samaki's neck, near the shoulder, but his jaws closed on only a fold of very loose and supple skin. Samaki meanwhile had struck at Matata's neck; he made contact an instant after the two-year-old, when the older animal's head was down on his shoulder, so that Samaki bit from above, his canines driving against skin drawn taut by the other's arched neck. Samaki's teeth gouged flesh. Matata's next strike pierced Samaki's right shoulder, and his superior weight twisted the younger otter to the earth, where he rolled onto his back in a defensive posture. The contest was a short one; for both otters the movements were not more than serious, and far more forceful, reprises of the rough-and-tumble maneuvers of their play as cubs. Matata, however, had had several opportunities during the last two years to practice and refine his moves in real fights, and Samaki had not. When the chance arrived, Samaki thrust his opponent upward with all the considerable force in his arms, heedless for the moment of the pain in his shoulder. Immediately he twisted himself up onto his feet and sped for the river.

Now that he could propel himself with his hindfeet alone, Samaki began to notice the hurt in his shoulder muscle, but he kept on, until he had put a quarter of a mile between himself and the scene of his defeat. Here he hauled out at one of his occasional holts and rested. His own territorial feelings were still in formation, and he was as yet no match for the more aggressive otter who had bested him. The wound healed well enough in a week for Samaki to use the limb normally. In the meantime, he found it possible to hobble about on three legs and to compensate for the painful forelimb in swimming; unable to turn left by thrusting with his right forepaw, the otter would roll belly up, thrust with the left paw, and then roll right side up again. He caught fewer fish during this time, but between what he did manage to catch and some snails and frogs, he did rather well. No infection set in, and his return to health was rapid. Once during the week of recuperation Matata came upon him in the river, but it was enough for the aggressor that his vanquished foe fled downriver, and the chase was short and almost desultory.

The hippos moved along the river bed in graceful, slow-motion bounds, trailing their coterie of labeos behind them. Samaki threaded his way through the group, giving each as much distance as he could. He paused in his swimming occasionally to roll onto his back and look backward over his belly at the big beasts. He could use his right forepaw a little now, but he still felt a twinge when he forgot and pushed too hard.

Finding a holt in this new territory was not too difficult, but he slept uneasily the first night, with the scent of Matata lingering in the damp air of the hollow. Yet the den was a good one, and he remained in its vicinity until his shoulder was serviceable again.

A mile and a half further downriver a bull crocodile was making himself conspicuous. A female had cruised into his territory. She measured some nine feet long, large in this era of intense hide hunting, and she was the biggest and oldest female for tens of miles downriver. The male, older by far, was nearly twice her length, a little less than sixteen feet from his snout to the end of his tail. For two days now he had been lying part of the time just out of the water, jaws open. Every so often the jaws would open wider, to their limits, and from them rumbled a long, thunderous roar, deep and hollow, as if it issued from the recesses of a long tunnel. Sometimes the sound was short and sharp, but always it had a basso tone, wrapped in its own echoes. It was this

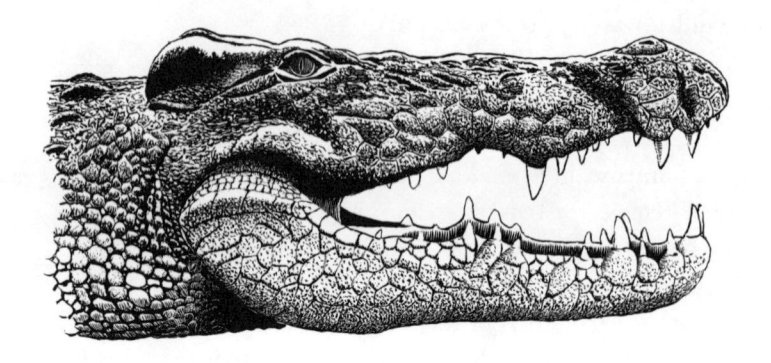

calling that had lured the female to the bull's domain, and when she appeared he slid into the water and moved silently toward her. They hung in the water, only their eyes, nostrils, and the bony ridges that housed their ears above the surface. It seemed as if these two living remnants of an expired age were lost in contemplation of one another for a long space of time, but perhaps some signal was passing between them. With the slow pomp of millennia in his movement, the male arched his spine in a crescent whose tips strained for the sky; the monstrous jaws rose from the river, parted a little, until they were fully exposed, while the tail arched up in a loop whose tip hung reluctantly below the waterline. Thus bowed, the crocodile sank slowly into the river, out of sight. But he had not yet played out his scene. His torso began to heave in a violent tremor, and a jerking shroud of bubbles poured from the corners of his mouth, erupting into the air in a tumultuous mass of leaping fragments of water. The massive head emerged again, higher, higher still, and then slammed downward to cleave the waters with a report like the sound of some large gun. Finally, the bull whipped his heavy tail violently from one side to the other; the river around him churned into a frothing soup of spray and bubble, the once-clear demarcation between atmosphere and water now a jumbled, ill-defined, and ever-shifting zone of no clear limits. His heavy, bony jaws clapped together again and again, each snap a sharp bang that has been described as the sound of planks being slammed together.

Faced with such an impressive performance, a female is as apt to swim nonchalantly away as to stay for the consummation of the ritual. But this female was ready to be mated. She moved to shallower water, where she could touch bottom. Her head and shoulders came up out of the water. Mouth agape, she raised her chin to the vertical and uttered a crepitous sound from deep in her throat. The male swam slowly up to her and heaved his huge forepaw over her shoulder. As she sank under the weight, he climbed upon her back, his tail twisting loosely with hers in a scaly embrace, his limbs clasping her. Two minutes later the reptiles separated.

～～

Samaki had the use of his right foreleg again. He had detected no trace of Matata or any other member of his species, except for an occasional stale and dissipating scent of that male on some exposed rock. He set out in earnest to explore the river, to see how far he could range before meeting another settled male.

The river widened considerably a little way down. It

grew shallower as its water spread, and a large island diverted the flow into two channels. Samaki followed the smaller of the channels, the northern one, and he passed the long island without encountering the big crocodiles, who lived along the wider flow. But there were other creatures—towering, wrinkled, fan-eared elephants, milling about on the bank. Even the two calves were giants to the low-slung otter, but they fascinated him as much as the hippos did. He could not see them as clearly in the air as a leopard might, but their bulk was difficult not to appreciate, and their waving ears held his attention for a long while. Their ropelike trunks were not so easy to make out, except that the variety of movements of these indistinct appendages registered well enough. In twos and threes the elephants moved down the shallow embankment to drink and to spray water over their red ocher hides, darkening the dust to a film of mud the color of brick. So intrigued was the otter that he almost forgot his hunger for a large part of an hour.

He treaded water watching, swam downriver to peer from another angle, then moved back against the sluggish current to see from upstream again.

One large cow shambled downstream past a clump of high papyrus out of his sight, and Samaki, almost unable to resist, dove and snaked his way through the growth, surfacing once for air. He swam near the bank, which in this place rose in an almost perpendicular wall for the space of perhaps a hundred yards. And there, before him, waggling slightly, was an apparition that caused him to check his forward movement and hang in the water, watching intently. It hung down from the surface two or three inches, a snakelike thing two-thirds as wide as his own head. Two eyes, or things that looked like eyes, peered straight forward from between two short, tapered fingers. It disappeared up out of the water, and while Samaki hesitated, not sure he should follow it up, it reappeared and dangled before him. This was too much to resist. He had not yet encountered a large snake, so he had no real fear. When confronted by some new creature that has made no threatening move, an otter—and many other animals, too—will often test it by a quick nip and withdrawal. If nothing untoward ensues, another nip or two or three will follow, and then, barring a counterattack, the otter will proceed to test the ease with which the new creature can be subdued, and its edibility. Samaki's head shot forward, and his teeth closed momentarily on the strange object. But the thing jerked up before he could open his jaws enough, and, one upper canine caught in a fold of the skin, he was pulled upward. In the process he freed his tooth, but the power of the thing's withdrawal had started his body moving up, and he bobbed out of the water as far as his chest. An extremely agitated elephant cow was hover-

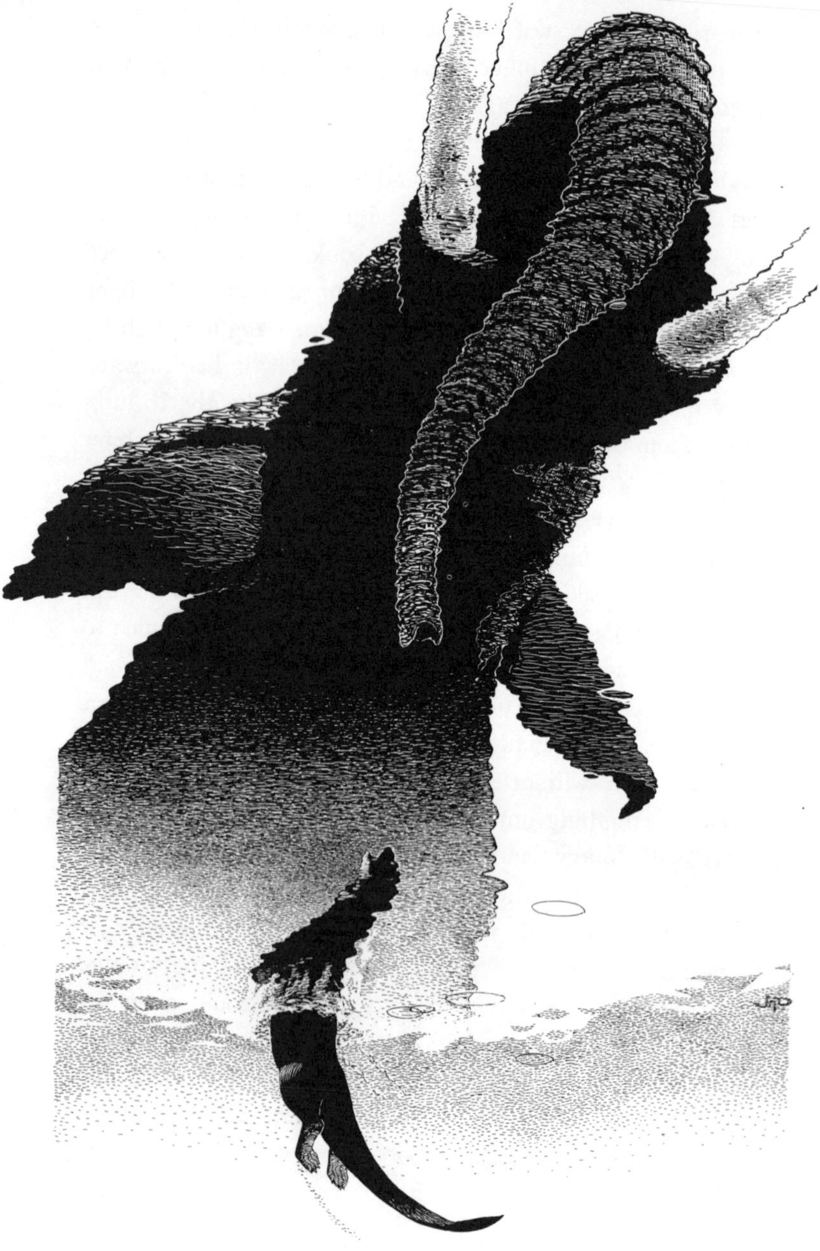

ing over him, as startled as he. The elephant and the otter each recovered from the mutual fright at the same time, the cow trumpeting and charging as the otter turned and streaked for deeper water. The elephant plunged down the short, steep drop into the water, stumbled, regained her footing, and crashed forward until she was up to her chest in her own turbulence. She halted, ears fanned out, blaring her upset and anger like a dozen trumpets blatting out of key. She scanned the water for her supposed tormentor, but Samaki was deep below, still fleeing. When he came up for air and looked back, seven other cows had materialized on the bank behind the angered one, who was now making her way back out of the water. For the otter several memories, fresh and distant, came together; he understood all at once that the largest of animals, whether elephant or hippo, were to be treated with caution, and if one day he came upon a rhinoceros, a species as yet unknown to him, that generalization would be applied to the rhino as well.

    Still shaky from his encounter with the elephant, Samaki sought a place to sleep, forgetting, in the excitement of the morning, that he had not eaten. When he awoke in the late afternoon, he was ravenously hungry. He slid into the water, found a small tilapia quickly, caught it easily, and ate it greedily, without bothering to haul up on the bank. It took away the cutting edge of his hunger, but it was not nearly enough to dispel the emptiness. He ran a minnow into the shallows and consumed it lying in an inch or two of water, but still he felt the need to eat. The next two fishes eluded him in a weed bed of some extent, and after probing in the green tangle without flushing more than a pill-sized beetle, Samaki kicked softly, and with a gentle undulation of his body, set himself drifting slowly and almost inertly over the crown of the weeds. Ahead, at the edge of the plants, he saw a fish.

The movements said "catfish." It was stouter and blunter in the head than the kinds Samaki was accustomed to, and it had something of a color pattern. The fish's silver gray back and sides—they had a pinkish cast, but the otter couldn't see that—were flecked with black spots, and there was a dark bar just forward of the tailfin. The fish had no dorsal fin, where a sharp spine would be found and was

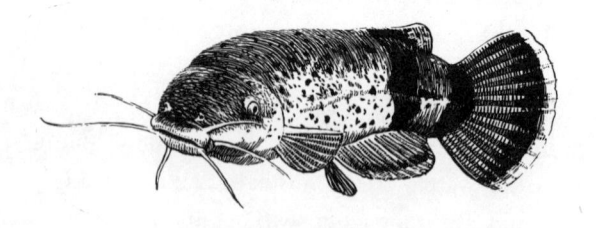

to be avoided, but the small, fleshy adipose fin characteristic of the catfish was there, just forward of the tail; the belly, like that of any other catfish, was pale. The creature wasn't large, no more than six or seven inches long, but it would make an adequate meal. Its attention was occupied with a smaller fish, which it was swallowing as the otter first spied it.

Push! With a coordinated thrust of both hindfeet, Samaki launched into a glide that brought him within range of the final spurt that would hurl him to the catch. The catfish remained where it was, so Samaki let himself glide to within less than two feet of it. He felt a touch of the mild wariness that always preceded an encounter with something new, but he recognized the thing before him as a kind of catfish (that ability to generalize had once again come into play), and catfish, he knew, made good eating. The quarry turned slightly toward him, hovering just above the river bottom. Samaki began slowly to bunch up all four feet for the forward kick, but it never came.

A terrible agony engulfed him. His legs jerked convulsively inward against his body with a force that would leave them aching later; his head rammed backward, compressing his neck; his lungs emptied explosively, wrenching a garbled scream from his larynx. He doubled up, tail lashing forward, and hung there in midwater, numbed, as time halted and consciousness flickered. Below him a stream of turbulence following the sweep of his tail raised a lazy swirl of silt from the bottom. As the pain ended, only an instant later, but before its cessation registered in his brain, the muscles of the otter's body, independently of his volition, spun him around and sped him away from the scene. Samaki gained control quickly, some distance away already, surfaced, and hungrily gulped in air. He floated for a minute or two at the surface, catching his breath. He had been assaulted by some unseen thing that brought pain of a kind and magnitude utterly alien to his experience. Before, pain had been something that happened at a definite part of his body—a sharp stab on the foot from a bite, a jab in the side made by an underwater snag passed too closely; a nip on the face from his mother, or a bumped nose caused by collision with a rock. This pain had enveloped him totally, everywhere at once, as if he had been slammed and bitten simultaneously from every side and from within as well.

Electricity, some two hundred volts of it, had been generated under the skin of the catfish. Like the electric eel of South America, to which it is not at all closely related, the electric catfish has evolved a spectacular means of defense unknown in terrestrial species. It can emit several strong pulses before exhausting its batteries, so to speak. It has been suggested that the catfish may use its power to stun prey; its use in defense is well established.

An otter does not dwell successfully on an injury; Samaki's attention turned easily to the remembrance of the fleshy-whiskered morsel he had been about to catch before the jolt disabled him. Dipping his head into the water, he propelled himself forward and down in a slow loop and roll that left the water surface almost undisturbed and positioned him, belly down, headed in the general direction of the catfish. He neared the place where last he had seen the fish, but it was gone. Catfish are not fast swimmers. The otter knew that, and knowing it initiated an unhurried cruise of the area. Just as he sighted his prey a little distance from where it had been before, he was convulsed by another shock, perceptibly weaker this time. His retreat was more controlled now, and he quickly doubled back for another attempt at approach. But now an elaborate caution dictated his movement. Slowly, hesitantly, he moved toward the catfish. He moved forward only inches at a time, braking and backwatering with widespread webs, and when the next shock came he was almost prepared for it. In fact, he had expected it and was testing that expectation. He was satisfied now that this oddly patterned catfish meant pain. He would never again approach, past the point of recognition, an electric catfish.

The sun was down before Samaki ventured into the water again to fish. The electric fish had dampened his spirits considerably, and he had spent most of the afternoon that remained curled in a hollow beneath a rock in the bank. In his sleep the day's two excitements had been replayed, separately and in an odd amalgam. He had re-enacted in his unconscious mind the playful bite at the gray trunk; he had been lifted again from the water, seen the enormous bulk against the sky, seen the widespread ears, heard the trumpeting, and sensed the charge that followed. He had felt the sting of the small speckled catfish, convulsed in sleeping body as well as mind. And he had fled a towering, spotted fish with flapping ears—or pectoral fins—that bellowed brassily and filled him at the same instant with unbearable hurt. He watched the bank warily as he fished in the night, and he felt a great relief when once again he was safe in the den. The following morning, when he saw an elephant at a distance, Samaki experienced a dread that was a carryover from the nightmare, and thereafter he accorded all elephants a respect far greater than was appropriate. He would always fear these lumbering giants more than any otter should.

CHAPTER 10

The next months in the vacated territory on the Mazingira were far from idyllic for Samaki. The elephants became commonplace, if sporadic, neighbors, to be viewed from a distance only, and the otter found it was no longer safe to doze under the cover of shrubs or out on the bank. The elephants had a way of arriving silently, their footfalls softer than a cat's. Once, as he napped on a rock that jutted from the bank, Samaki was awakened by a snuffling blast of air almost in his face; a half-grown cow elephant had come upon him and, uncomfortable about passing by the small carnivore, had given him a gentle, but unmistakable order to leave. He complied with ungraceful haste. Another time his awakening had come under a bush, to the sound of branches being torn and twisted off by a large, muscular trunk. The elephants accorded him a benign disdain, and Samaki more than willingly deferred to them. Soon he took to napping on the matted wads of dead stalks within a bed of reeds, but the elephants occasionally intruded into the fringe of the reeds, and he had to seek out more secure holts.

The holts he found dug into the bank were not particularly well worked, what few there were; this part of the river, isolated from human traffic as it was, and well supplied with fish of large size and a relative abundance of antelope, was too well suited to crocodiles to allow long-term tenancy by otters. It had been occupied over the years —perhaps centuries—by young, newly independent otters, who had become grist for reptilian jaws or, if they were lucky enough or quick enough of wit, had moved on to safer havens. Because of this, no den had been occupied long enough to have been scraped and worn into the sort of snug, flood-proof, comfortable resting place Samaki had found elsewhere.

While Samaki haunted the northern channel, the two large crocodiles remained chiefly in their territories along the southern passage—the female tending her clutch of buried eggs, and the male relatively sedentary because of the easy supply of prey in the larger flow. Within the first week of his arrival in the vacant otter territory, Samaki, on a ramble along the south bank, had caught sight of the male, and thereafter he avoided the area. Once the otter happened upon the female, in the early days of her three-month vigil at the nest. She was not in any way incubating the eggs, but she remained within a few yards of the place where the eggs lay beneath the ground, ready to drive off any monitor lizard or civet that might seek to exhume the clutch. From time to time she would slide into the river to wet herself and then return to drip over the nest site. She had no interest in food, nor did she stir herself to drive off any but the most persistent egg thief; her very presence discouraged most would-be marauders.

Samaki came to know where the mother crocodile was likely to be and, after a few sorties into her nesting area, was able to move about with caution, unmolested. There was a danger that this crocodile's inertness might allay

some of his fear until, her young hatched, she once more resumed her predatory life. But Samaki had already had his close call with a younger crocodile, and his memory was long; his mental image of the brooding female cast the vivid shadow of his cubhood encounter, and he never passed near the saurian without half expecting her to leap into activity.

The male crocodile, Samaki found, had fairly regular times for basking—on the sandy south shore of the island in the mornings and on the steeper south bank of the river in the afternoon sun. It was possible to invade the nearby waters at these times, but such an endeavor was risky business; in time, his calculations might be faulty, or the reptile might modify his timetable. By the sheerest luck the otter discovered that the male passed the nights in the water; twice his bulky form had loomed dark and ominous ahead of Samaki, fortunately facing away from him. And twice was enough. Samaki avoided the crocodile's territory thereafter when the sun went down. The crocodile, of course, never missed the otter. He required surprisingly little food for his bulk, because of his relatively low metabolic rate. The river abounded in fish, some very large, and at times he snared an antelope come to the Mazingira to drink. He was a hunter of opportunity, and rarely did he seek out a specific prey.

The crocodile was not the sole agent of death in Samaki's part of the Mazingira; a leopardess paid calls at the river sometimes, but usually she sought easier prey than the otter. She wanted a small antelope, but would not have ignored an otter that made a target of itself. Samaki was appropriately cautious and survived.

Only once their lives drew nearly together; Samaki had hauled out on a mud slope to eat a six-inch labeo. As he chewed noisily on the fish, a domed head, tawny and dappled with black, rose with imperceptible slowness over a jumble of rock seventy feet inland. The leopardess made herself as small an object as possible. Her ears drooped low, changing her usual outline, and she rose above the edge of the rock only to her pale, gray gold eyes. She had heard the sound of the otter's jaws. Her tactic, so effective when her prey was an antelope or a hare, was hardly necessary now, for the otter's distant vision would not have disclosed her in any event. She gathered herself for the leap and charge, shuffling her hidden hindfeet restlessly; her tail twitched sporadically. Samaki, meanwhile, had consumed the fish, and as the cat hunkered down the better to thrust herself upward and toward the otter, Samaki slipped casually into the water and submerged. He saw nothing of the aborting charge, and when he surfaced the leopard was gone.

The river and its environs still had things to teach the otter. As the rains of April began, the crocodile's brood hatched. The female had left her station, and Samaki was somewhat disquieted when he made this discovery. There had been a certain comfort in finding the big reptile always in the same place, and now the status quo had changed. For several days Samaki crept quietly around the periphery of the nesting area; his curiosity prompted him to search

for the creature, but vivid recollection of the threat she represented tempered his investigative urgings, and for a time he avoided the vicinity completely. Instead, he frequented the north channel, where the elephants represented at least a known entity.

It was late morning. The last of the giants ambled off into the distance. When he was sure they had gone, Samaki worked his way up along the elephants' track. He paused often, testing the air with nose and ears, and watched for movements that signaled danger. Nothing appeared to be out of place, and he continued up the slope, away from the river. A small movement drew his eye; down the slope toward him came a creature of a sort he had never seen before. It did not scamper. Neither did it scurry or slither, hop or crawl; rather, it rolled, and humps appeared on its outline, only to disappear and come into view again. Two giant dung beetles were rolling a ball the size of a hen's egg built up of elephant manure. Male and female, they were rolling the ball, pushing it and riding up over it, searching for a place, a certain kind of place, with qualities only a dung beetle could know, where they would inter their sculpted sphere and where the female would lay her eggs.

Samaki inched toward the tumbling ball, stretched to his limit.

Although the beetles labored mightily to move it, the globe of dung's course was determined in part by the minor irregularities of the terrain and the slight, but insistent, pull of gravity toward the base of the slope, with the net effect that the sphere wobbled uncertainly as it went. It halted and bobbled, shifted direction without preamble, and was possessed of an unpredictability that both fascinated the otter and fanned the embers of his caution. At last, when his muzzle was only a breath away from the ball, it lurched abruptly and soggily against his nose. Samaki drew back, turning the smell of the fermenting manure over and over in the nostrils of his mind. His paw reached out, fingers spread, and bowled the thing, skittering, to his left. One beetle, dislodged, lay on its back, flailing six legs futilely in the air, but the second rode its careening treasure until it bumped to rest against a grass clump. Samaki swerved from his intended pursuit of the dung ball to poke at the kicking beetle on the ground. He shied away as two thrashing legs grazed his whiskers; then, eyes squinting, he minced at the beetle with his incisor teeth. Brittle legs snapped away, rendering the insect utterly harmless, and two bites more opened its juicy thorax. He ate all but the hard covers of its wings, then turned again to the dung ball, which he licked delicately and tentatively with his narrow tongue. Its taste he found to be not at all repellent, but a taste was enough. The second beetle caught his attention as it tried doggedly to set the ball in motion again, and he took it deftly in his teeth and ate it. For the next ten minutes he played with the ball, batting it and pushing it with his nose; his play was vigorous, too much so for the loosely compacted material, and it left bits of itself plastered on stones and plant stems, until it fell apart into fetid chunks. The game was over. In time each fragment would support microcosms of bacteria and fungi, very small beetles, and other lesser invertebrate creatures; and the molecules that had once been parts of plants, the molecules that had not become parts of the elephant, would, by a complex chain of transmutations, become parts of plants once more and then find their way into another herbivore's gut—another elephant's or an antelope's or a mouse's. Some would again pass through, undigested; others would become flesh, only to be appropriated into the body of a carnivore, but the cycle would play itself out endlessly, so long as animal life survived along the river.

Through the months of April, May, and June the crocodile mother guarded her young. The little ones stayed together, hiding in reedy vegetation, scouring the shallows for aquatic insects and small tadpoles, dispersing wildly when a large animal drew near. But always they reassembled, and always the big female was nearby to drive away the herons and marabou storks that came to prey. Often the hatchlings basked on the half-submerged trunk and tail of

their mother, safe from the many dangers of a world filled with larger predators. But when they passed into their fourth month the members of the brood began to seek solitude, and their mother's bond to them was already weakening rapidly; a year or two from now she would in all probability view them as prey, if they met again.

July was a month of crocodiles. The female was prowling again, and Samaki's freedom of movement narrowed considerably. But then there were the hatchlings; of seventy-nine eggs, sixty-eight had given up their living occupants. Nearly sixty of the infant reptiles still survived, the others having been eaten by storks and a large catfish. One blundered into the grip of a large crab. The survivors had moved along the river, keeping mainly to the reedy areas, and clawed small tunnels into the bank. Samaki took his toll of the brood. Some he encountered in open water or during his sorties into the reed beds, but he learned, too, about the tunnels and how to gauge the times when the miniature crocodiles were apt to emerge. The storks and other predators were active, too, and the ranks of the hatchlings thinned rapidly.

Each time Samaki sensed the presence of one of the two old crocodiles, he grew increasingly restless. Another otter—and most of his predecessors were like this—might have hung on doggedly to the territory, accepting the crocodiles as an inevitable part of the world, but Samaki was acutely conscious of their menace; he had already dealt with their species. A second factor in the otter's discontent was loneliness. Normally one or two females would be found within a male's territory, but his home range was sterile in this respect. Nor did he find any male companionship. The usurper, Matata, quarrelsome and stronger, held his old stamping grounds just upriver, and he had not yet encountered a male to the west.

On a morning in the last week of July Samaki roused himself from a nap on the bank. His belly was still pleasantly filled with the flesh, bones, and scales of a tilapia. A restlessness filled him, and for two days he patrolled his neighborhood as though driven. And indeed he was. When he played there was a near fury in his movements. He hunted more often, eating less of each catch and leaving generous portions for the scavengers.

On the morning of the third day, Samaki had just made a successful catch. The chase had not been a demanding one, and the small catfish, still jerking spasmodically,

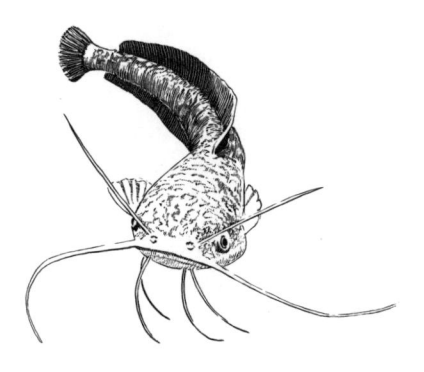

lay where he had dropped it on the coarse sand of the bar. Its smell was particularly enticing, and the otter lost no time in biting a chunk from its middle. He tipped up his chin and chewed the soft flesh noisily; fish juices trickled down his gullet. Holding the body between spread forepaws, Samaki bit off another mouthful. He never noticed the large grain of sand that adhered to the fish, and it was now within his mouth, lost in the midst of the flesh. Samaki chewed on, shifting the meat from one side of his mouth to the other alternately. The mass shifted, shifted again, to the left side of his mouth, enfolding the foreign object until, *crack!* A small tooth just forward of the large, blade-like carnassial tooth, driving upward to meet its mate, rammed against the diminutive stone and split neatly in half from crown to root. The otter yelped, but otherwise was unaware of what had happened. When he resumed chewing he felt the sand grain and he spat it out with the remainder of the chewed fish. Then he took most of the mass of fish meat back into his mouth, leaving the sand.

Because this time he chewed on the right side of his mouth, things went well; but when he moved the meat leftward again, the halves of the cracked premolar shifted slightly, and he felt pain. Not a serious pain, but enough to be uncomfortable, and he made certain after that to chew on the good side only. It involved some trial and error, however, for the pattern of shifting his food was not an easy one to break, and only after several reminding twinges did he adapt to the new state of affairs. Later Samaki caught and ate two small fish, played a bit in the water and on the bank, and retired to his holt to sleep.

Toward the end of the following day eating became even more uncomfortable. The left lower gum had begun to swell. By the next morning any movement of his jaw hurt; Samaki was ill. He had no desire to leave the den, but he was uncomfortably hot lying there. The fleshy pads of his paws burned, and the relief he gained by pressing them against the cool earthen walls of the chamber was slight. Always before, when strenuous activity raised his temperature, the water on his paws had cooled him. If his activity had taken place in the river, his naked palms and soles conducted that heat to the water, and if he had heated up on land he would plunge into the river or sometimes merely dabble about the shallows. An otter, whose underfur must remain dry, can ill afford oozing sweat glands that would foul the woolly layer, and the naked parts of his feet have evolved to use the waters of his world as a cooling agent.

Samaki rose to his feet slowly, groggily, and took himself to the river. He eased himself into the water and floated almost dreamily. The coolness soothed his paws. He swallowed some of the water—it was not easy to do—and, something he had never done in good health, defecated as he floated. His stool, loose and mixed with the normal mucous secretions of his gut, floated to the surface and some adhered to the fur of his flanks before dissolving and floating away. But enough remained in the fur to lessen its resistance to the water, and when the otter returned to his holt, parts of his hindquarters were abnormally wet.

During his next fitful sleep the otter's jaw swelled further, and the swelling invaded the tissues of his cheek and neck; a week after the tooth cracked Samaki's face was lopsided and grotesque. In the interim he sought the water often, and when hunger became unbearable he prowled the muddy shallows where he found worms and other creatures slow enough to capture and small and soft enough to swallow without chewing. In the past this sort of prey had been only for snacks, but now it meant survival. The worms were simple to catch, but other forms of life—tadpoles and small fishes—moved more quickly than his retarded responses could cope with, and he took few for the energy he expended in pursuit. Only through luck did he not encounter the crocodiles or the leopard on his forays. Had his path crossed any of these, he would have been easy prey.

He lost flesh rapidly—more than a pound, a twelfth of his weight, in a week. The reduced intake of food and water brought dehydration. His system fought the infection with a singleness of attention that brought other functions to a halt. His urine became concentrated and the production of oil in his skin nearly ceased. Each time Samaki left the water his fur was wetter than before, and this, combined with his almost total omission of self-grooming, left his fur ratty and matted, smeared with mud from the den.

Time and the otter's adamant constitution conquered the infection. The swellings subsided by the latter part of the second week. The fever left, and Samaki awoke one afternoon with a reborn interest in living. He was weak. He was hungry. But even more, he wanted desperately to feel himself hurtling through the river in pursuit of a fish. His first fish, a tilapia, was too quick for him. He tired rapidly and turned his attention then to frogs and worms. Twenty minutes later, while he was chewing a small frog, the two halves of the broken tooth were dislodged, and he swallowed them without knowing it. Before half an hour more passed he had eaten nearly as many small creatures as he had in the entire week before. His fur was in poor condition, but back in the holt he began again to groom it, spreading the loose skin between his forepaws and nibbling delicately with the incisors that were set between his fangs. Swimming continued to tire him for several days, but each exercise brought strength and each meal added substance to his wasted frame. The first labeo Samaki caught filled him with a sense of exultation, and thereafter fish were a part of his fare. The oils in their bodies broke down in his digestive system and recombined as oils in his skin; his fur began to shed water effectively again, and twenty days after he had cracked his tooth Samaki was once more sleek and efficient, with leisure to play and to exercise his boundless curiosity.

The restlessness that had animated him just before the accident returned in force. He stretched languorously in his holt one morning late in August, just as the eastern sky was bleaching into day, left the chamber to find breakfast, ate, played with the empty shell of a land snail on the bank, and dozed for an hour. When he awoke, he slipped into the Mazingira and swam westward with the current to patrol the downriver border of his territory. At the border a log floated slowly downstream, and it evoked images of the two large crocodiles. Samaki hauled out on the bank and trotted westward; he had left his home to seek a better place.

CHAPTER 11

For nearly two months Samaki traveled down the Mazingira a distance of eleven miles, to the point where the Hama River emptied itself into the larger flow. This last stretch of the Mazingira was much like the part in which he had lived in the shadow of the crocodiles. Hippos inhabited the lower reaches in small groups, and a few elephants visited its banks. Antelopes of several species were common, as were zebras, and giraffes gazed down from against the sky. Crocodiles were few, the result of intensive hide hunting, as they were these days few throughout most of the African continent. Within a few miles of his point of departure he came upon a female otter, Kiwete. Half of her right hindfoot was missing, the two outer toes and the tip of the third sacrificed to a six-foot crocodile six months earlier downriver, along with the last inch and a half of her tail. She walked with a barely perceptible limp, and when she ran the normal humping gait of an otter was more pronounced, as she kicked off more strongly with the left foot. She was a trifle overweight, owing to her tendency to swim less than is usual for an otter. The swifter fish of the Mazingira were beyond her capability to catch because of her disfigured foot; she could not push through the water as strongly as she had when both feet were sound, and her steering in a chase was impaired by the reduced surface area of the injured foot. She had learned to approach her prey whenever she could from the left, her good left foot able to steer her toward the right for the final lunge, but most of her food now came from shallow water, where she could kick with both feet against the river bottom. She ate frogs and small crabs, snails and millipedes mostly, and in season plucked ducklings down under the surface. With such easy catches her expenditure of energy was minimal, and since her appetite

had not diminished, her body had converted the protein surplus to her needs into a layer of fat.

Kiwete saw Samaki climb up on a river rock to dry, and her amicable nature drew her to him without caution. He started when her head broke the water a few feet from his resting place, but when she hauled up, burbling, he relaxed. The two meshed whiskers, then played out the ritual of mutual sniffings and nosings. The female had always been unusually trusting, ingenuous, a quality that has small survival value for a wild animal, and Samaki was so starved for companionship that he quickly overrode his natural wariness.

The wrestling games in the water fulfilled a strong need in both otters, but in the long chases Samaki found his companion too easy a mark. He had been aware, during their greeting ceremonies, of the oddness of Kiwete's right foot, but he made no connection between that and her relative clumsiness in the water. He did learn to compensate for her reduced maneuverability, however, and his chases were more restrained thereafter; it had been less than an hour after their meeting before Samaki made the adjustment.

When next he hunted, Samaki subdued a large tilapia and brought it to the rock. As he chewed his first mouthful Kiwete inched over and sniffed at the fish. Eagerness to taste again something larger than a morsel balanced precariously in her mind against a high degree of reticence about attempting to eat from another's catch; her side began to itch insistently, and she escaped her dilemma by scratch-

ing. Samaki had not warned her away when she was near, she realized as she scratched, so she stopped and inched close again, eyes upturned and fixed upon him. Again there was no warning. She reached out furtively and bit off a small chunk. She chewed as rapidly as she could and swallowed her booty. The next bite was a bigger one that required her to hold the fish down with one paw, and again

Samaki made no move to thwart her. She grasped now the fact that this male was not like the only other one she had known, and the remainder of her meal she ate without fear. When Kiwete sought her den later in the day Samaki followed her, and the two slept, crowded within.

The first fish of the afternoon was a small labeo, barely four inches long, and Samaki held it between his paws as he ate. His response to Kiwete's approach this time was a low growl, and she respected the sound. She slid into the water to seek out small, soft-bodied things. Samaki's next fish was a big catfish, and this he allowed her to share. Within two days the female came to realize that the size of a fish governed the male's attitude, and she ate of his prey then only when it was big enough. Samaki never sought out large fish deliberately, but a sufficient number of them fell to his agility and speed to provide frequent feasts for the bitch.

The arrival of the resident male broke the idyll. Samaki avoided him as far as he could, but there were encounters. None were as bitter as those with Matata had been, and the other male never deliberately sought Samaki out. But Samaki was always defensive when they met. He lacked the confidence of possession, and by mid-September, less than a week after his second birthday, Samaki set off again down the river. In the third week of October he reached the Hama. The rains, meanwhile, had set in; at times they were extraordinarily heavy, and Samaki laid up wherever he could find shelter more of the time than was usual. The Mazingira, swollen and brown, made hunting more difficult, too, so that he needed more time to get his accustomed ration. The Hama had overflowed its south bank in places, creating broad swampy areas that harbored a multitude of frogs and small fish, so the hunting in the floodplain was not at all bad. There were hippos here in numbers and a few crocodiles of fair size. The otter turned north after spotting the third crocodile, and in the narrower channel, above the confluence with the Mazingira, he found no crocodiles.

Flooding on a familiar stretch of water is something that can be coped with; an otter knows where the rocks lie in the river bed, where the fish of each species are likely to be found, and where the safest holts are. Here, in strange territory, Samaki found life stressful. When the rains ended in the early days of November, and not long after that the Hama moderated, his interest in the area underwent a resurgence, but something about this stretch of river did not sit well with him.

Samaki left the den at daybreak. He caught two fish, poked about the copse of fever trees near the bank, found three big pill millipedes, and ate them without much enthusiasm. An appetite of another sort had begun to infiltrate his mind. An image of Kiwete, a combination of vague visual image and a crisp olfactory one, interrupted the everyday images of swimming and basking and toying with pebbles. He heard the phantom of her burbling welcome, and with it came a place memory of the smells and sounds of the part of the river where she lived. A memory resided in his body, as well, composed of the feel of certain paths along the bank, the slopes of hauling-out places of rock and earth; and he had a sense of its position higher on the Mazingira. The image pulled at him, and he found himself moving down the Hama toward its junction with the Mazingira. When he had traveled nearly a mile, Samaki left the water and, with due caution, crossed the flat, sandy bank to nap under a low shrub. He dozed.

Samaki's eyes blinked open, and his head shot up from the duff in stiffened alertness. The sound that had taken away his sleep was a steady growl, like a waterfall a little. But waterfalls grew slowly in the ear as one approached, and this grew suddenly, while he moved not a yard. It had something, too, of the quality of the indistinct stiff-winged things that passed high overhead on rare occasions, although its drone was softer.

It became louder still, and yet louder, until the otter felt a compulsion to leave his couching place in the thicket and make for the river. He did not hurry, but loped with easy strides down the slope, across the few feet of damp sand, and into the river. He directed his course some thirty feet upstream to a clump of reeds and lost himself among the stalks, where he could wait, unseen, for whatever came.

The Land Cruiser had been given a coat of green paint in the Japanese factory where it was built, but Africa had given it a coat of red ocher dust that disguised the green as effectively as it hid the gray of an elephant's skin. The car growled over the near horizon and pulled up a hundred yards or so from the bank. The growling stopped. From his hiding place Samaki could not see the four figures emerge, but their voices reached him, and he stiffened. One figure was a black man dressed in khaki trousers and a faded plaid shirt that gave to his exposed arms and face an even darker hue by contrast. He was a wildlife biologist, schooled at the University of Michigan more than a world away, and he looked as if he might be more at home in some large suburb on a Saturday morning. He was speaking to a white man dressed in a floppy cloth hat of khaki, pants of the same material, and a sleeveless bush jacket that did not quite match and whose pockets bulged with cannisters of film, tape cassettes, and a miscellany of other impedimenta. His tanning face was framed in a scruffy beard, dark gray where it grew from his chin, silvery on the cheeks. His years of overseeing the care of animals in a large zoo, without having to engage in the more physical aspects of the operation, had added more weight to his frame than was seemly; the shortness of his stay in Africa and days of travel in the Land Cruiser had given him little opportunity to walk. A woman followed, slender and dark-haired, in a muted green bush suit and a broad-brimmed Australian-style hat, looking every inch the tourist; a camera hung on a strap around her neck. She turned and helped a fourth figure, half her size, from the car. The last, a little girl of not quite four years in khaki shorts and bush jacket, carefully carried an Instamatic camera she had just learned to use; the film, when developed, would yield photographs of half a cow, a defecating village dog, and numerous blurred landscapes taken from the bouncing car. Her long sandy hair was shielded by an oversize bush hat like her father's. She and her mother followed the two men down the slope toward the bank.

The woman stopped to photograph a small flower, and as she did the little girl hunkered down to gaze raptly at an iridescent beetle crawling up a stem of grass. At the river the men parted, eyes to the ground, and drifted in opposite directions along the bank.

"Over here!" the black man called. "Here's a leopard's print in the sand!" The bearded man took half a step toward the otter, hung uncertainly for an instant in midstep, and stooped over quickly; his eye had caught something of more interest to him—five small prickmarks in a fan-shaped pattern in the sand.

"The leopard'll have to wait, Winnie. I've found an otter print." He squatted and lifted his camera, now resting on his paunch. He focused, adjusted the settings of the lens, and took three photos at close range. Then he set the camera's aperture wider and shot two more pictures, as insurance. He stopped down the lens then below the original setting and prepared to make two more exposures, but after the first the film would not advance.

"Damn. I'm out of film," he remarked, to no one in particular, and rewound the film into its cassette. He removed it and placed it, almost tenderly, into its small aluminum cannister, screwed the top on carefully, and stuffed it into one bulging pocket of his jacket.

The black man walked up, looked dubiously at the faint marks the white man pointed to, and then the two searched for other prints. But they found none and drifted over to where the leopard had been. Samaki watched their movements, unseen.

About halfway to the cat's pugmark the bearded man paused and leaned over to peer at what he had at first though might be another otter print. The last film canister tumbled from his pocket. A tuft of grass muffled its landing, and it rolled further down the slope, coming to rest against a stone. The men walked on, examined the leopard's mark, and left to join the woman and child, who were still scrutinizing the foliage where they had first stopped. They all had many miles to travel before dark, so the quartet boarded the Land Cruiser, and in a roar of low gear the vehicle disappeared.

When he was certain these strange creatures had gone, Samaki slithered out of the reeds to investigate, in his turn, the footprints the men had left behind. These prints smelled not at all like the tracks of other beasts; they held the alien scents of oil and the ghost of asphalt and the not at all subtle fruitiness of a small girl's bubblegum that had fallen to the floorboards of the car and subsequently wedged in a cleated sole. The otter inhaled these strange odors avidly, not knowing quite what to make of them, until the water lured him back.

He halted in midstride, his eye caught by a dull glint off to his right. Could it be a fish? When he reached the cannister, its satin aluminum finish fascinated him. It smelled like no fish; rather, it had an animal scent, more like a baboon's than a cat's or an otter's or an antelope's. He pushed the can with his nose; it rolled an inch or two. He pushed again, then batted it sideways with a forepaw. He kept the cannister in motion for a minute or two, until it skittered at last into the river, where it floated a little more than half below the surface, the capped end lower than other. A shove with his nose sent the toy bobbing away, and Samaki slid into the water after it. He submerged, rolled over, and came up with his chest under the can; two rubbery forepaws darted out and grasped the can. The otter righted himself and kicked his way toward the river bottom, clutching his prize. When he slackened his hold, the film cannister shot toward the surface. Samaki followed and snatched it again. Like a bit of bark, it sought the ceiling of the river, but it bobbed up more quickly, as if, almost, it had its own will. The feel of the cannister was strange, however—hard as any pebble and smoother than most, but pebbles always sank. The unexpected combination of the container's qualities intrigued Samaki more than any inanimate thing he had come upon before, and he played with it for a longer time than usual. Its shell gave sometimes when he closed the vise of his jaws upon it, but more often it simply deflected his canines. Once he was able to mouth it in just the right way, and one canine pierced it with a sharp little sound and an odd scratching sensation in the tooth. When next he pulled it down, minute bubbles of air trailed from the can; and when he released it, it was in less of a hurry to rise. Not long afterward his jaws stove in the part that fitted into the cap, and air rushed out. The cannister of film had become a stone in behavior now, as well as in feel, and the otter's interest in it ebbed like the flow of the river. The can sank to the bed of the river and came to rest in a small puff of displaced silt. The emulsion was softening, the latent image of Samaki's pawprint and of fragments of the lives of other animals disintegrating, never to be seen. In time silt would cover the cannister, as it covered stones and waterlogged twigs and the bones of creatures that had met their end in the river.

It had been but a minor distraction, and now Kiwete filled his mind once again. He trotted down the riverbank, then dived into the flow, and let the current help him on his way toward the Mazingira.

CHAPTER 12

Spurred by the memory of Kiwete, the otter consumed the miles of the Mazingira's course in a few days, relentlessly, except for an odd dalliance here and there with a pebble or a shell or a seedpod. Near the end of his quest, Samaki's first encounter with the female's spraint quickened his pulse and then his pace, but it was more than an hour until he found her, holed up in her holt for the midday rest. Her perfume was strongest at the entrance to the den, but he entered cautiously just the same; from deeper in the tunnel her anxious "Fff!" met his ears, and he chirped a reply.

Kiwete had not yet fallen asleep when she heard the footfalls and detected a darkening of the dim light that meant something had invaded her burrow. Alert, she issued her alarm exhalation and readied herself to fight if she had to. But Samaki's chirp, its pitch and timbre, identified him, even after his months of absence, and she rose to her feet to meet him. A taste of his scent preceded him by an instant, confirming his identity. Kiwete burbled her hello, a sound born of her pleasure. To Samaki the voice identified her and conveyed at the same time her good mood. They met in the tunnel a little beyond the nest chamber.

A flood of mutual pokings and sniffings tried to erupt in the tunnel, but the narrowness of its bore confined the otters' attentions to their faces and necks. Samaki pressed forward, trying to force his head past Kiwete, without success. She backed toward the nest chamber at his relentless pushing, and once within the larger place they completed the ritual, nosing shoulders and flanks, chests and genitals. Samaki drew deep draughts of scent from the female's groin, and she in turn from his; his scrotum pinched upward reflexively at her touch, drawing his testes up to the abdomen. At length Kiwete groomed Samaki's shoulder with delicate nibbles, and he reciprocated. Greetings concluded, the otters slept.

For three days the reunited companions hunted, slept, and played together. Samaki's old willingness to share his larger prey manifested itself again, and the plump female devoured the unaccustomed food with obvious relish. But halfway through the afternoon of the second day, some small circuit within her shifted its pathway. In the midst of a tussle in the river, she whipped her head around and snapped at Samaki, chittering as she did. He lunged at her playfully, but she repulsed him again. Samaki withdrew and found business elsewhere until, a half hour later,

Kiwete bobbed to the surface near him and invited a chase. Before they retired for the night, she had driven him away twice more, only to regain her composure within minutes.

On the fourth day Kiwete met his morning greeting with a rebuff; she chittered at him as he poked his muzzle into her shoulder and struck at him. She was coming into heat. Her irritability was not nearly as pronounced as Maji's had been when she had made her transition into estrus, because Kiwete was by nature of a more even temperament, but the irritability was there. For Samaki the change in the female's demeanor was of little consequence compared with the change in the way she smelled. To his sensitive nose there came now a new quality in the bitch, a something that excited him and brought on the beginning of an erection. The new scent overlaid Kiwete's familiar perfume or, more accurately, pervaded her musk, making it different, new; and at the same time, her scent was the same. There is no way to tell if Samaki's response to the change in Kiwete's scent involved an awareness of what was happening within him or if it was purely a blind effect of an instinctive urging, a chemical command to his nervous system triggered by chemicals that emanated from the female. Whatever its origin and mechanism, however much or however little Samaki understood of the things that were taking place, matter not at all. Two changes were indeed under way, one in Kiwete and the other in Samaki, and the interests and activities of the pair were shifting dramatically.

Kiwete's flashes of irritability passed as swiftly as they began. They bewildered her in a vague way; if she could have reflected on them the way a human does, she might have feared for her sanity. But she could not dwell on her changes of mood, and the bewilderment was always short-lived, displaced by her old desire to join her companion a small distance away. Her chemistry was changing, as estrogens seeped into her bloodstream, and the hormones were setting her nerves temporarily on edge. When she sniffed Samaki, on rejoining him, she began to detect a new quality about him, and on land it was even more evident. The maleness about Samaki had changed little, if at all, since his return, but Kiwete's burgeoning femaleness was sensitizing her to it. In the next days, when she was not bickering and snappish, she found his groin increasingly fascinating. The musky scent of his genitals was becoming no longer merely one of the many odors permeating his fur, but to her an increasingly powerful and exciting signal. She inhaled the evaporating scent of his urine, too, with an intensity she had not known, and it held a significance for her that was at once strange and unsettling, and yet seemingly familiar. Although she could not understand its significance, she knew it in her viscera more surely by the hour.

Samaki, too, was disturbed by the change in Kiwete. Her mercurial irritability confused him, but it stirred within him some near-memory of his mother's outbursts at Mto. Yet he had in the time of his youth been only a bystander, and the memory never quite came into focus. Within him, entwined with the confusion over the female's passing savagery, there grew an intensifying new dimension to his interest in her. Her scent was changing, becoming more demandingly female. For Samaki it was not a metamorphosis of anything within him—not yet, at least—but a true reconstitution of the other animal. Resting on a rock he felt his penis swell beneath his abdominal skin, but the odd sensation had not thus far linked itself with any definite appetite. More and more, however, the swelling followed upon his detection of that disturbing, almost hypnotic scent that centered between Kiwete's hind legs. And more and more Samaki's nose was drawn to that place. Kiwete would stand as he wedged his muzzle under her rump. And at times so directly and so intently did he investigate, that he lifted her rear quarters until her feet hung in the air.

For days the female's mood swung from snappish to affectionate, and she kept Samaki very much off balance. There were times when she approached him to poke her nose with great deliberateness against his throat. Samaki

responded to these advances by raising his chin as high as he could and holding as still as a statue. Whether Kiwete's perusal held any menace is difficult to say, but the male's behavior suggested that the investigation was a solemn and serious one.

On the third day and night after Kiwete's transformation Samaki sought out a separate sleeping place, although he could not keep away from Kiwete during their active periods. Morning of the fourth day brought an amicable

Kiwete again, a Kiwete almost coquettish. She burrowed her muzzle now under Samaki's hindquarters, under his tail, his genitals. Samaki rolled onto his right side and lifted his left hindfoot as she probed, filling her nostrils with his male scent; then, shaking her head slightly, she trotted away and slipped into the river. Samaki followed.

Under a lowering afternoon sun the otters separated to search for food, Kiwete poking in the shallows and Samaki cruising to deeper water. A minnow, which he ate in a few bites while treading water, took the edge off his hunger and, in fact, seemed to eliminate any further desire for food. He patrolled the vicinity, remembering the crocodiles, but his attention was divided; the vision—or more accurately, the scent—of Kiwete surfaced insistently in his head. Had one of the large crocodiles been in the vicinity, he might have fallen to it, but the reptiles were at the cores of their own territories, still basking in the waning heat of the sun.

The otters met in the water. Samaki slipped his muzzle under Kiwete's tail, lifting it clear of the river and inhaling her scent. She was utterly receptive and permitted him to glide over her back. In some species of otter, some females are quarrelsome in the extreme during the mating process, and some males equally aggressive, but for Samaki and Kiwete the mating was almost tender. Rarely did the male grasp her nape in his teeth, as so many members of the weasel family do. He clasped her rib cage in his forearms, not very tightly, and pressed his ankles, considerably more firmly, against either side of the root of her tail. He entered her.

The two otters floated, joined, for perhaps half an hour. Every so often Samaki's pelvis thrust spasmodically, and from time to time Kiwete would pirouette slowly beneath Samaki's chin. As she twisted he loosed his hold on her thorax, but the hold of his ankles never slackened, and he twisted with her, still joined. Some time after they had

uncoupled, Kiwete, for no apparent reason external to herself, lashed out at her mate, nipping him painfully on the neck. As the river darkened, and crocodiles would be abroad, the otters left the water. Samaki had eaten little in the past hours, but he was not yet hungry. He trotted behind Kiwete for a space on the way to her den, until she wheeled and chittered at him. He retired to his own holt, alone.

In the morning Samaki sought Kiwete in her den, but she had already left. He stayed some minutes scrutinizing the scented earth where she had slept before returning to the river to find her. She snapped at him, chittering, as he swam to her, and then she paddled to an exposed rock and hauled out. Samaki drew near again, and now she held still while he nuzzled her throat, only to bite at him moments later. But the male persisted, and soon Kiwete groomed his neck, poked her nose against the corner of his mouth, returned again to his neck, and worked her way backward along his flank. Samaki in turn perused his mate, pausing longest at her turgid vulva, and then the two slipped into the river. Here, Kiwete submerged and resurfaced with her nose in Samaki's groin, and for some time after she flirted with him as they lazed in the water.

They copulated again late in the afternoon, this time for well over an hour, Samaki maintaining his grip on the root of Kiwete's tail with his ankles. When they separated and came to the bank for a rest, Samaki became absorbed in his own genitals, their own odor, and that of the female that lingered on them. Kiwete maintained a distance from him. His approaches became more tentative as she met him each time with a bickering chitter and ready jaws. Later she welcomed him again and submitted willingly to his poking about her neck.

For three days more the pattern was much the same, bouts of prolonged mating, always in the water, alternating with interludes in which Kiwete was peevish at her best and savage at her worst. Most carnivores mate with an in-

tensity that is almost ferocious—some North American otters in coitus leave the impression that a violent rape is under way. Others of the same species are more gentle in the act. Samaki was a gentle animal. Most of the time he and Kiwete were joined he spent gazing absently into the distance, his only movement the short thrusts of his pelvis. Only once did he grasp Kiwete's neck fur in his teeth, and his grip was a soft one.

But his mate's mercurial changes of temper were having their effect on the male. Successful mating requires of a male otter that he endure these flashes of hostility with an equanimity he might not possess at other seasons. Samaki never fought back, never returned a bite for a bite, but meekly suffered each attack, and when circumstances warranted, left his tormentor for a time. Yet he was not nearly so indifferent as his outward nonchalance might suggest. If humans did not suppress anxieties and hostilities without being aware of it, there might be no psychiatrists in the world—or any need of them. The animal mind and the human are not so different as traditional scientific and folk opinion hold; however much they may be set apart in terms of complexity, whatever seeming qualitative difference the human ability to verbalize may have introduced, their disparate lineages were once a common one, and the emotions of both have unwound from the same skein. Because an otter cannot rationalize as a human can, its capacity for psychic distress is far less; but the otter's flesh is heir to many of the same heartaches and natural shocks that afflict a Hamlet.

Samaki's response to his inner turmoil was more elemental than that of most humans and its cathartic effect swifter and more complete.

Several times during the otters' week of mating Samaki's pent-up inner ferment exploded into a frenzy of mindless energy. At these times he would leap into the water, as in a panic, his belly thwacking the surface, and churn forward some distance, his movements shifting to a wild and seemingly uncontrolled porpoising. The overwrought rush ended so abruptly that only the damping disquiet of the water remained as testimony to the event. Samaki would be calm again now, as much within his marrow as in his outward demeanor.

Once, before his internal pressure had had time to force the escape valve, Samaki, quietly scanning the river from a resting place atop a slab of rock, was startled by the sight and crash of a branch, eaten too far by termites, in the riverine forest. He flung himself into the river and swam, most of the time submerged, for many minutes. After reemerging onto the rock, he stood erect, head cocked slightly, and stared nearsightedly toward the source of his upset, spluttering excitedly. In contrast to his bursts of pure, spontaneous activity, this upset died slowly and reluctantly, and its cleansing effect was imperfect. Under normal circumstances the crash of a limb, by no means a rare occurrence, would scarcely have aroused his curiosity, and then only briefly. A hundred yards further along the bank, nearer to the falling limb than Samaki was, Kiwete stiffened for an instant, cast a glance over her shoulder at the source of the sound, and relaxed again.

Kiwete's sexual attractiveness waned gradually, and her shrewish disposition returned to its normal amicability. Samaki's special interest in the female dwindled, too, and as it did his appetite returned. What little weight he had lost during his rutting he regained quickly. The otters were no more than occasional companions again, but it was enough. December had just begun.

CHAPTER 13

In the fortnight following their breeding Samaki and Kiwete met nearly every day and sometimes more often. Their meetings were cordial and their play relaxed. Three eggs, fertilized by Samaki's sperm, had begun the process of cell division—two cells, four, eight, and onward, until each took on the appearance of a microscopic, translucent raspberry; then, still floating free in the uterus, each developed a hollow center. At this, the blastocyst stage, they implanted themselves in the uterine wall and began to shape themselves into crude quadruped form. Kiwete carried on her life as usual, unburdened by the morning sickness that marks the early days of human pregnancy. Complex chemical changes were in the making within her body, but if she was aware of the processes, her behavior gave no witness.

Chemical changes, orchestrated with equal complexity, had been under way for five months in another female, the one of reptilian lineage. The she-crocodile in the broad south channel of the Mazingira, gravid with her cargo of nearly completed eggs, lost interest in her usual routine and reoccupied the old nesting site she had used for so many years. Her breeding cycle, and that of the males, had been finely programmed through millions of years of trial and error in the ancestral line to assure that the eggs would be laid and incubated in the dry season. Her kin in other parts of the continent bred at different times of the year, each in concert with the seasonal periods of downpour and dryness, and except when the rains were premature, each raised clutches of young, most destined to be fodder for the lesser predators. When she had been in residence for a few days, she scooped out a chamber in the earth with her hindfeet. Some fourteen inches below the surface she extruded eighty-three eggs and covered them for their three-month incubation. She would maintain a vigil now, eating little and leaving the vicinity of her nest seldom, and then only briefly. She might seek shade when the sun grew uncomfortably hot, but she would never be far from her investment in the future. For Samaki and Kiwete the crocodile's dedication to her unborn young made the river a safer place. In the waning days of January Kiwete grew restless and irritable again, but it was a new kind of irritability, a sort she had not experienced before. Her abdomen had been swelling; the four teats between her thighs had been lengthening, swelling, until they were no longer hidden in her fur. The tissues of her mammary glands were changing in character, cell upon cell readying themselves to draw minerals, proteins, fats, and sugars from her bloodstream and combine them in the proportions best suited for the growth of her expected cubs. She visited her several holts until she settled into the one that felt most right. She was not consciously seeking the deepest or the driest or the one nearest the shallows where food was abundant, but somehow, through some unconscious racial wisdom, or perhaps only by luck, she found the best of the available places in which to couch her young. Samaki again was confronted by a fury, but this time the virago's behavior was untempered by any sexual lure, and he avoided her after very few rebuffs.

Kiwete brought three cubs into the world on the second day of February: two robust cubs, a male and a female, and a second female, the runt of her litter. With a deftness that belied her innocence of motherhood, she removed the amniotic membranes and placentas, nipping the umbilical cords near each baby's belly, and she consumed the afterbirths with unpracticed greediness. The male cub, only minutes old, raised his blind head high into the air and, still damp from the maternal fluid, squalled a complaint against the unpleasantness of the external world. It was a lusty, but reedy cry, and it awakened in Kiwete a concern that overrode all other aspects of her life. She nuzzled the cub and then his littermates, brought them nearer, and soon all three discovered her teats.

Samaki made one more attempt to see his mate. He dawdled uncertainly near the entrance of the den and, hearing a cub's cry, let curiosity cancel his caution. But he had not gone far into the den when he heard the now-familiar chittering response and then a menacing growl that rose in pitch until he retreated.

Restlessness overtook him, seeping into the void left by Kiwete's antagonism. He began moving upstream, into his old territory. There he detected the perfume of two females, but no male. His tree holt had been slept in by one of the females, but no rival had moved in. One of the females was a yearling, friendly, but shy, and the other an older animal, not much inclined to play. The old tree holt was as he had left it, and he adopted it once more as his principal home. It was situated near the downstream end of the territory, no more than three or four miles from Kiwete and her cubs, but he stayed within his old domain, content with the occasional meetings with the two resident females; he had no urge to return to the hellcat he had left and her attacks. Upstream, as he patrolled his beat, he encountered signs of the neighboring male; the latter's scent marks extended further downstream than they had before. Downstream Samaki's territory bordered the one he had left, vacant of another male, and after a few weeks of meeting no evidence of a neighbor, he began to expand his patrol further downriver. It was no deliberate expansion of empire, no planned move, and it happened almost by chance. When he found no musky declaration of ownership at the edge of his range, he poked about a few yards or a few hundred yards further downstream. Sometimes his excursions brought him to a stretch of bank where the duff was pleasant to dry himself in or to a rock that caught the warming sun just right. Or the tangle of branches of a fallen tree would prove to be the haunt of tasty fish. Each of these amenities prompted him to return, and little by little he nibbled away at the no-man's-land beyond his old borders. The absence of crocodiles large enough to be a threat added to the attractiveness of the newly annexed areas. By the middle of March Samaki was regularly exploring territory not far from Kiwete's old den, although he had not added so much of the river to his claim as a permanent matter. Yet, the nearer he drew to the old holt the more his apprenhension grew, remembering, as he did, Kiwete's attacks. Slowly his curiosity and courage grew, entwined, but when at last, remembering the pleasant side of his mate, as well as her hostile aspect, he inched his way to the mouth of the den, Kiwete's scent was faint and stale. She was no longer there. Detailed inspection of the den confirmed it.

He turned his attention to his right hindfoot. The fourth toe, injured by his old bout with the crocodile, had lost some of its ability to flex; its tip set higher than the other toes when he walked, and its claw was not being worn away at a rate equal to the others. The claw had elongated in the past months, and its feel disturbed him slightly, especially when he used the foot to groom his fur. Bending and tilting his head, Samaki lifted the foot and inserted the abnormal claw into the side of his mouth, where his carnassial teeth, designed to slice through flesh and small bones, nipped bits from the claw until it felt right.

Kiwete had moved her month-old cubs nearly two weeks ago to another holt over a mile farther down the river. Why a mother otter will do this, no one knows; perhaps the urine of the cubs makes the earthen floor intolerable. Perhaps the mother suspects the presence of a predator in the vicinity or of an interloper of her own species too strong to repulse. Perhaps a den suited for bearing young and rearing them in the weeks of their infancy is no longer adequate as they grow larger. For whatever reason, move them she did, hauling each by the scruff or cheek or throat, whichever was most handy, the long distance to their new home. She hauled them sometimes through the water, sometimes on the bank. At times a cub would hang limply, to be dragged as dead weight; at other times it would lollop along on its hindlegs, forequarters held high by its mother. The first cub to be moved, the larger female, squalled piteously when she waited alone, in an alien chamber, as her mother returned for her second baby. Reunited, the two would cry less vigorously in each other's company, while the last youngster, abandoned without her littermates, took up her paean of distress. As young cubs will, the little otters adapted readily to their new surroundings, especially once their mother was with them and when, in her absence, her scent permeated the holt. But Kiwete, who had lost part of her foot and the tip of her tail to a crocodile, had brought her offspring nearer to the two big reptiles. Only the midriver island separated her holt on the north channel from the bony-plated monsters in the south channel.

A span of three days in the third week of March

snatched up Samaki's life and forged it into something other than it had been.

In the morning of the first day Kiwete left her cubs and went to the shallows to seek the invertebrates on which she depended for sustenance. The growing cubs' escalating demands on her ability to produce milk had drawn heavily on her excess fat, and she felt a need for greater quantities of food. The shallow waters yielded little in the way of nourishment this morning, so, still hungry, she made for the island, and not yet sated, rounded it into the south channel. The sun was high, and the male crocodile, growing hot, had slipped into the water to cool. His hunger had gone unabated for a long time, but he was not hunting. Yet this otter was too easy a target to ignore. He was upon her before she knew it.

By nightfall of the second day the cubs' hunger had become acute. They called for their mother, toddled restlessly about in the holt and to the edge of the fearful unknown that lay beyond the entrance. They fell, one by one, into a fitful sleep, sucking for comfort upon the tails or feet of one another.

Well before noon of the third day, the female crocodile, sheltering from the sun under a patch of shrubbery, heard the beginning of a subterranean chorus from her entombed brood in their nest some sixteen yards distant. The "Ao, ao, ao" of their yelping stirred her, and she moved ponderously to the nest site and began to scrape away the sun-baked earth that imprisoned them. She clawed chunks of soil that had been compacted by her weight and fired by the solar heat, soil through which the hatchlings might never escape unaided. She took occasional clods in her jaws and gouged carefully with her teeth until she was near the squawking young. Popeyed and wet with the fluids in which they had grown, the little crocodiles began their climb to the surface. Particles of earth adhered to them, and those that tumbled back on their exodus emerged at last looking as if they had been rolled in breadcrumbs in preparation for the feast that most of them would soon join as unwilling morsels.

Samaki, meanwhile, had passed the island, heading downstream in the north channel. He had dined, crossed to the south bank, and was now returning up the river in the direction of a holt he knew some distance farther upriver from the crocodile's nest. He had seen the big female on the same nesting site when he had lived here with Kiwete; he remembered where it was, and as he approached the area he kept well to the edge of the stream, avoiding the place, some fifty yards inland, where he expected the beast to be.

As the newly hatched crocodiles clambered to the top of the excavation, the mother picked each one she could find gently in her jaws and with a slight flip of her head, tossed it into her maw. She depressed her broad tongue to make a kind of pouch of the floor of her mouth, and each baby, as it settled into the warmth of this haven, changed its anxious yelping to a softer sound. At times the young emerged more rapidly than she could gather them, and some wandered off, still calling. When she turned to search out a straying baby, others would crawl from the nest and in turn become separated from her. The culmination of her long vigil was keeping her busy, and although she had scarcely eaten in three months, and had lost considerable weight, the young presented no stimulus remotely resembling prey to her; her mouth and jaws were maternal organs now.

Samaki, trotting along the bank, avoiding the nesting site, had focused his attention in the direction of the nest. He emerged from some underbrush a few short yards from the crocodile, on her way to the river. Had he not stopped he would have collided with her midsection. The mind of a crocodile is still an enigma—it may be that the sight of the otter rekindled her memory of food, or she may have recognized in him a threat to the young she could no longer see, but could feel resting in the distended pouch of her mouth. She could not attack him successfully without endangering her brood. In all probability she did not actually know this, but something in her genes did, and that something would protect the small ones. The old crocodile whipped about and would have grazed Samaki, at least, with her snout, had he not dodged backward, spluttering. Had the reptile opened her mouth as she swung her head, her infants might have been jettisoned. Some of them, at least.

So she kept her mouth closed and hesitated just enough in launching her attack to render it ineffective. But so far as the survival of her species was concerned, bringing her offspring to the river was the necessary deed, and the loss of one animal that might be prey for her or predator to her young in the future mattered little. Samaki dashed to the river and waited motionless until he saw the enemy slide into the water. As she opened her jaws to let the babies slither away, Samaki crept up the bank again and proceeded up the river's course with renewed caution. He remembered, too, that the male crocodile was likely to be basking somewhat farther along the bank, a recollection sharpened by the incident with the female. He kept under cover as much as he could, and paused frequently to reconnoiter the path ahead. And he was acutely alert to the small sounds and half sounds around him.

The middle of the day was approaching, and the otter felt the need to take his customary rest; the image of the crocodile lunging still in his head urged him to add more distance first. This was not familiar country to Samaki, for although he had been here before, its reptilian tenants had precluded it as a place in which to stay or sleep, and for this reason he had no special resting place in mind. He sought some sheltered spot in a thicket, where an approaching enemy would create enough noise to give warning. And so far he had found no such place. He maintained his careful pace, but a lifetime of daily siestas had begun to drain his energy.

Ahead, a toppled tree slanted down into the river, barkless trunk bleaching in the sun. Often such trees had deep cavities, Samaki knew, and he moved forward to investigate. Nearing the tree he heard small splashing sounds, sporadic and complex, as if more than one creature made them. They were not crocodile sounds, nor turtle sounds, nor bird sounds. He did not consciously attempt to categorize them, but in his brain some mechanism scanned the catalog of memory for a match. A plop reached Samaki's ears, and he identified it easily as a frog, just at the point

when the other splashes were crystallizing tentatively into otter sounds. Then a reedy chirp, and the identity of the splashers was no longer provisional. Quickly, but still cautiously, Samaki rounded the jagged disc of roots and earth and saw the cubs.

Three little otters, bellies slack, were poking in the shallow water. Too young to have left the holt with their mother or to know about the practice of hunting, they were simply responding to the motions of diminutive aquatic creatures in retreat from the disturbances they made. To their myopic eyes movement was an attractant, and in the course of a purely playful pursuit, the nipping that followed brought a taste of food. Given time and no inopportune arrival of some large predator, the cubs might learn to feed themselves, and perhaps one or more might survive. Samaki moved toward them, but before he had taken half a dozen steps the cubs raced toward him; thus far they had known only Kiwete, and Samaki's indistinct form meant only one thing to them.

Samaki, on the other hand, somehow recognized them as otters and as cubs and braced himself for the leaping that would follow. He was not prepared, however, for their frantic search for maternal teats, and he leaped backward with the clumsiness of surprise. The cubs in turn were startled, first by the suddenness of Samaki's leap and then by the dawning recognition that this "mother" had the wrong smell. Their eagerness deflated for the moment, they were still enough for Samaki to investigate each with his nose, until he had satisfied himself that they were indeed otters; they held the additional fascination of having something about them that was Kiwete. That recognition flickered briefly within him, and then there was no time for more, as the cubs assaulted him with their affection. Samaki joined them in a wild, tumbling romp, all thought of sleep vanished.

But twenty minutes later, as the cubs tired, Samaki's sleepiness dropped upon him again. He found a suitable cavity in the trunk, and, followed by the cubs, he padded into it, alert for any danger within. Moments later all four otters were asleep.

Samaki awoke several times in his two-hour sleep to the disconcerting feel of small muzzles poking his groin, but he rolled over each time and lapsed into sleep again. The last time it happened he found all three cubs awake; the two that were not seeking to nurse were chewing on each other in mock battle. He was hungry, and so were the cubs.

The little ones followed their guardian out of the hollow tree, dogging his heels, but stopped when they were less than belly-deep in the river. Samaki paused to survey the stream, then slipped quietly into the water and disappeared, much to the distress of the cubs. They stared out toward where he had disappeared and they chirped their abandonment.

At the age of six weeks the cubs' pelts were no longer the gray mousy color of infancy, but were chocolate brown, and their throats now had a definite pattern of spotting. Mgono, the male, favored Samaki; his throat bore a complex light pattern—more saffron than white at his age—which enclosed a few brown blotches. The larger female, Kipaku, had a broad whitish yellow band from chin to chest, overlaid with a freckling of brown. Kuliwa, the smaller female, more nearly resembled her brother and still had a few tufts of grayish baby hair scattered over her body. The three waifs dithered about on the edge of the river calling loudly, but Samaki was submerged, in hot pursuit of a small labeo, which he seized in his jaws. He surfaced, treaded water, and consumed the fish in a few bites. He heard the shrill chirping as he ate, but he had none of the instinctive sensitivity to the sound that a mother would have had.

A large catfish fell to him in the next few minutes. It was a big fish, nearly half Samaki's length, but it was slow, and once he had severed its backbone he was able to manage its bulk easily. As he did with all large fish, Samaki hauled it to shore to eat. The cubs bounded over to him joyfully, but he was still hungry, and hunger increases an otter's sense of proprietorship; he growled, and when Mgono, the male, approached to investigate the object he did not yet know to be food, Samaki hurled a bite his way. The bite was a mild one as otters' bites are measured. A bite with full force would have driven canines through a cub's skull and brain—it can penetrate thick shoeleather—but this bite had little force; Samaki's mouth was not opened far enough for his fangs to be of any use, and only his incisors met on the cub's cheek. A pinch, but pinch enough to be read as chastisement, and Mgono pressed himself to the ground. When Samaki resumed his meal the cub slinked away.

Sated, Samaki left his fish, and Kipaku, and then Kuliwa, inched over to it investigate; Mgono took longer, expecting at any moment to be rebuffed again. But Samaki had no further interest in what was left of the catfish, and the cub's confidence grew. None had yet tasted fish or even smelled it on Kiwete's breath, but hunger had given them a desperation and a receptivity to anything made of flesh, and in no time at all the three were gorging themselves on the soft tissues. Their digestive systems were still geared for a diet of milk, with its specific proportions of fat, protein, sugar, and minerals, but they would be able to make use of the fish. Their rate of growth would not quite be as expected, but in later months their development would adjust—if they survived the other hazards of their youth.

While the cubs glutted on Samaki's leavings, their father returned to the river to swim for the sake of swimming. The cubs were in no mood for play when he returned; bellies filled, they sought only sleep, but when Samaki led them further along the bank they trailed behind him. He searched out a dense patch of brush and led them in. There he scooped up a pebble, rolled onto his back, and juggled it desultorily, while the cubs snuggled close and fell asleep. Before many minutes passed, Samaki, too, grew drowsy, and the pebble tumbled to the ground.

CHAPTER 14

Samaki awoke, stretched, yawned, and stretched again. He had changed position several times in his sleep—if it was indeed truly sleep. He had dozed, but even then his ears had remained open to suspicious sounds, and he had raised his head at irregular intervals, triggered by a shrew's collision with a brittle leaf, again by the fall of a twig at last rotted through by fungus, by the shrilled alarm of a small bird frightened by a small mongoose. Each time, satisfied that no danger was near, he relaxed and slipped into semi-unconsciousness. The cubs fell into the deep slumber of the naive, adjusting to the dislocations caused by Samaki's vigilance without waking. Samaki had already forgotten his encounter with the female crocodile. The memory of it remained, however, stored out of mind, waiting to be evoked if the future should summon it. Stretching and rolling, the otter felt a small pressure on his rib cage. He shifted, idly scooped up the offending pebble in the rubbery web of his left paw, and rolled it onto his chest.

Kipaku opened her eyes, spied her brother, stretched, and pounced upon him. The ensuing tussle quickly expanded to include their smaller littermate. For the moment they had no thought for Samaki, who, absorbed in the tactile pleasure of juggling the pebble, accorded them only a small

part of his attention. Not far upriver the male crocodile stirred.

The crocodile moved slowly, stealthily. He placed his feet carefully, keeping to the open area where sparse grass was the only vegetation on the floodplain. He was watching for movements, listening for betrayals of movements unseen. He paused often. He was hungry again, but he had learned from his years that hunger must be abided if it is not to be compounded. None of the crocodile's knowledge had been acquired on a level remotely conscious, of course, but had been accreted, synapse by synapse, as sandstone is built of individual grains. No matter at what primitive stratum of the mind the knowledge had accumulated, it was an education as true as the schooling of a human child, as enduring, and as vital to the deadly earnest business of surviving in a threatening world where his own error loomed as the only real danger other than man.

The saurian's progress, unhurried, relentless, brought him in a few minutes to the audible limits of the cubs' scuffling, just as a sharp yelp of juvenile pain punctuated the river's soft sounds. The crocodile's pace quickened, even as the little otter forgot her pain and reapplied herself to the fray. The tempo of his footfalls increased steadily. Soon stealth transmuted itself into speed, soft steps into pounding thrusts. He had a clear bearing on the cubs, and now he plowed forward, heedless of the crashing of brush yielding to his bulk.

This new sound jerked Samaki to his feet. An anxious "Fff," low in volume, but sharp, escaped his mouth and froze the cubs in midtussle. His second ejaculation was rougher, almost a splutter. A pause for a brief inhalation, while the otter reared tall and straight as a post, eyes and ears focused toward the rushing noise, nostrils flared. Samaki spluttered—a rough, fricative rush of air as harsh as any sound that comes from a living throat. He was already in motion. He had recognized the danger, and lacking the emotional constraints of motherhood he had not even a momentary inclination to defend the cubs. For their part, the cubs, confused, responded blindly to the adult's alarms and to his sudden flight. They moved clumsily, and small obstacles easily cleared by a grown otter thwarted their efforts to follow him. All four otters bolted for the river, but by different pathways.

Samaki burst noisily through the roof of the river; in his panic there lingered no ghost of the fluid grace with which he normally melted into the stream. His feet flailed wildly while they still pushed only air and, once below the surface, drove him forward without stop. The air in his fur trickled out in a chain of glittering bubbles. The larger of the female cubs and her brother converged beyond a large stump; once their bodies brushed before Mgono drew ahead and plunged into the water just above a jutting boulder. Kipaku reached the river half a length behind him. Both heads bobbed to the surface sneezing water from their nostrils, and the two, scrabbling to keep their heads in the air, were eased around the rock by a sluggish eddy and bumped gently against the bank out of sight of the crocodile. By the time they had gained courage enough to clamber up the bank, the enemy was already past them.

The smallest cub reached the river's edge a couple of yards above the big rock. She summoned her flagging strength to hurdle a thick, twisted root, almost cleared it, teetered, and fell into the river.

Her unexpected plunge into the water compounded her panic. Her scrabbling brought her the better part of a yard from the shore before the buoyancy of the water lifted her feet totally from contact with the river bed and converted her terrestrial gait into an instinctive dog paddle. What little further capacity the cub had for fear was realized; for the briefest instant she paused. Clumsily she began to turn. Then, terrified by the sight of the onrushing bulk, less substance than a huge, inexorable motion, she redirected her flight toward the deeper water.

The crocodile churned onward, closing the gap between them with terrible ease. He slid into the water, pounding up spray from massive feet that propelled him through the shallows. As the water deepened, his legs almost automatically ceased their motion, folding backward to reduce drag. The powerful tail began to snake from side to side, slightly at first, then with increasing force, pushing him forward. He was in his element. A muscular flap in his gullet closed to seal out the water from his respiratory tract; the valves in his nostrils and ears closed as well.

The reptile's eyes never left thier target. Pupils closed by the sun to vertical slits tracked the small furry head, and as the giant lizard form slipped below the surface, they accommodated to the refractive change from air to water. Kuliwa now appeared as a headless thing, her feet scrabbling wildly in the milky brown, translucent field. The crocodile plowed on.

Twisting slightly onto his side, the monster gaped; deadly rows of bulletlike teeth passed forward of the otter's tail, then drew alongside her chest. Sensing the ominous presence, the cub, confused, paused in her paddling momentarily, and the dreadful jaws slashing to the side engulfed, not her middle, but her head. Two convulsive shakes of the reptile's head tore apart the tissues of the cub's neck. The headless body spun upward, to fall down to the water again a few feet away, bobbed briefly in the waves generated by the crocodile's thrashing, then slipped lazily below the surface. Small puffs of blood blossomed from its ragged neck, tinted the murky water, and dispersed into invisibility.

The massive jaws opened, lifted upward; the lifeless head of the cub half fell, half rolled down into the cavernous recess. The watertight seal that marks the boundary between mouth and gullet was open. The crocodile swallowed. In no hurry now, the reptile turned to take the torso. Almost daintily he grasped the limp form, again lifted his chin to the sky, and felt the warm body fall limply into his bony maw. He swallowed it whole. The memory of the other running, edible shapes transmitted signals down the spinal cord that sent his right foot out, spread the webbed toes, and concluded with a powerful kick that turned him counterclockwise, until his snout drew perpendicular to the shore. The muscular tail lashed left, then right. He spurted ahead, slowed, and drifted to the shallows. The quarry was nowhere in evidence. The crocodile waited patiently, inanimate. Something akin to disappointment flickered briefly in his diminutive brain and died. If the crocodile has a virtue, it is patience. Two objects that had been a young otter were already decomposing in his gut, reducing to compounds that would recombine as an imperceptible increment to the crocodile's substance. He waited for his next meal to blunder along.

The wait was not to be a long one. Samaki, spurred on by the crocodile's thrashing, had redoubled his underwater flight; but when the sounds ceased, his otter curiosity grew strong again. There was nothing to be seen at any distance through the silty water, so he surfaced and hung upright, maintaining his balance with slight adjustments of all four paws. Only the most insignificant of ripples spread from his emerging head. They dwindled rapidly as they spread until they spent themselves not far away.

Some fifty yards distant only the single bony boss in which the crocodile's nostrils, and the two in which the eyes and ears were set, extended above the waterline. Samaki scanned the surface, not yet aware of the deadly pattern, but one pale reptilian eye was even now sending nerve impulses to the primitive brain. They registered the presence of a small, rounded, dark object that had not been there a fraction of time ago. And it was turning slowly in a circle. The crocodile stirred imperceptibly. The three bony growths moved slightly against the weak current describing a lazy arc that would not have ended until they stopped, like three points placed on the apices of a spearhead aimed at the otter, had they not melted down into the surface of the water in midturn.

The otter spotted and recognized the moving pattern in the last moments of its visibility. If danger had appeared on the shore, Samaki would have dived with all the strength in his muscular frame, causing a splash that might attract an enemy's attention to the diving point, while he streaked away below the surface. This time he exhaled slightly and slipped, like a sinking ship, down into the murk. His bulging eyes hastily swept the field in the direction of the crocodile, but it was still too far away to be seen. Samaki kicked out repeatedly with his broad webbed paws, with all four, and his body undulated rapidly to add to the thrust, reflecting the movements of the crocodile.

Periodically the otter spun onto his back to scan the water behind him. Looking back over his chest he was less hydrodynamically perfect, but powerful kicks of his hindfeet kept him moving forward. On one of his scans he was aware of an ambiguous shadowy patch behind him, slightly to the left as he looked, and growing just noticeably larger. He braked with both right limbs and stroked with all the strength of his left paws, rolling as he turned, until he was again belly down. Thrashing his backbone, much as a porpoise does, adding this thrust to the strong push of his broad, webbed hindfeet, Samaki darted across the river.

When next he rolled to look backward, the saurian shape was more distinct. We do not know with what senses the crocodile tracked the otter's erratic changes of direction in cloudy water that rendered the smaller prey even less visible than the pursuer. But the crocodile did perceive his quarry and pressed on. Samaki recovered from his latest check behind him barely in time to avoid colliding with a large rock. The crocodile had been clearly outlined this time, three-dimensional now in the hazy water. The otter's quick reflexes sent him kicking away from the obstacle, then around it. In only slightly more time than this automatic motion required, Samaki's cerebrum reassumed control. He surfaced, wreathed in a silvery sheath of exhaled breath, gulped down fresh air, and dove to peer around the rock. It had been his first breath in nearly a minute.

The reptilian juggernaut had checked its speed with spraddled legs. For reasons perhaps known to the crocodile, perhaps merely by chance, the scaly predator veered to the upstream side of the rock. Seeing the enemy's direction, Samaki doubled up and thrust off from the downstream side, moving as speedily as his muscles allowed with the weak current. The crocodile lost precious moments relocating his quarry and still more heaving his sixteen feet of bulk through the ninety-degree arc of the new bearing. His vertically flattened tail gave the crocodile a more efficient

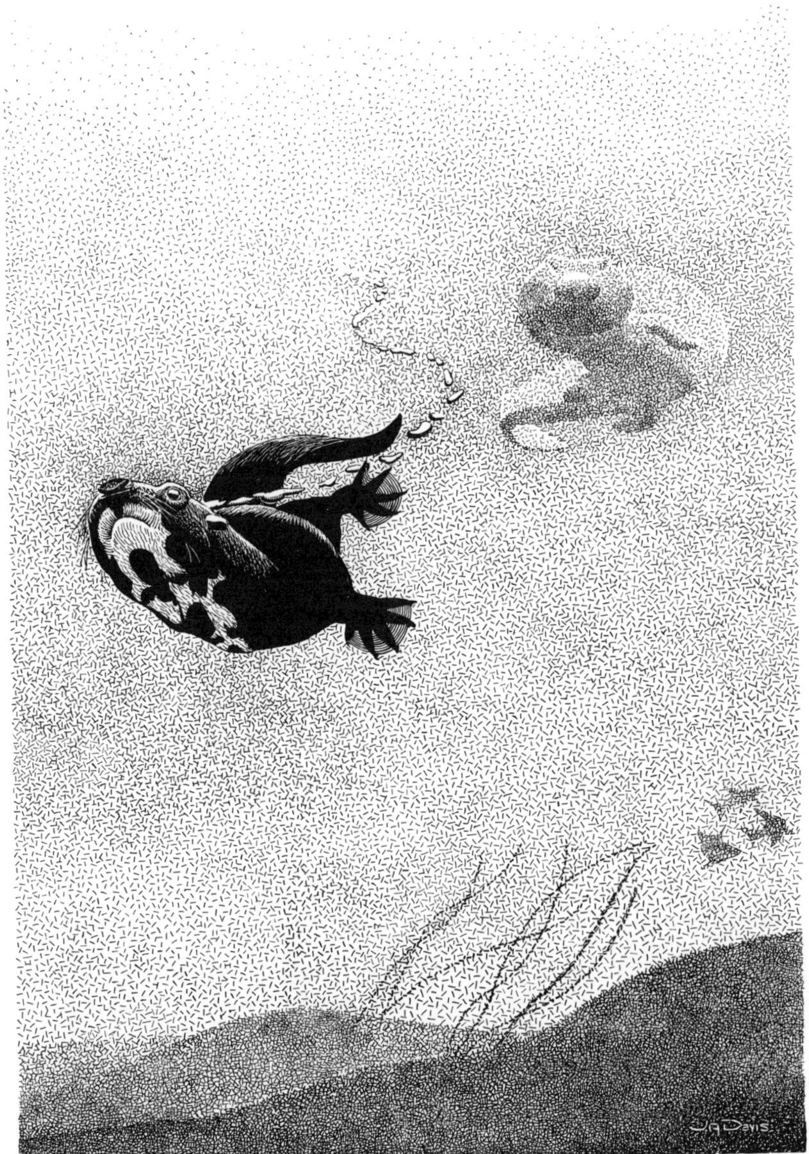

JG Davis

surface to push with against the water than the otter's horizontally flattened tail did, but the reptile's ton of bulk, with its enormous forward momentum, took a fearsome energy, and far longer time, to overcome than the otter's fifteen pounds, and the distance between the two increased for a time.

A malachite kingfisher, perched on a low-hanging branch on the bank stared with mild interest at the slight disruption of the surface where a chain of bubbles exhaled by the moving otter broke the water film. Then, nearer and to the upriver side of the rock, the water exploded, exposing a blur of lashing, plated tail. The bird rocketed from its perch and fled. On a new and higher perch it saw the otter's head break the surface, look about in haste, and submerge again, bound for a patch of reeds some fifty yards away on the shoreline.

In the comparative haven of the reed bed Samaki snaked his way, using paws and thrusts of his torso to propel him between the stalks. The water here was shallow; Samaki could float and still touch bottom, and he took advantage of the opportunity to breathe deeply as he hurried deeper into the vegetation. The crocodile, too, made use of the shallows. Head above water again he could see the otter's progress translated into movement of the reeds high over his head. He crashed forward, leaving a swath of broken, trampled stems in his wake.

Samaki, meanwhile, had run out of shelter, such as it was. He peered from the reeds, the crashing behind him growing nearer, then launched himself once more downstream. Ahead of him, where the water was deeper, he could see two gray brown boulders, one large, one smaller, just protruding above the surface. He plummeted toward them, aiming for the gap between, but as he drew nearer under the water the smaller bulk moved, and nearer still he made out the silhouettes of a hippo and her calf.

The big cow raised her head until, like a crocodile, her eyes and nostrils were above water. Simultaneously her mobile ears, also in air now, picked up the sound of the onrushing crocodile. They pricked up and swiveled in the direction of the reeds.

In a natural balance of power adult hippos coexist with even large crocodiles, and neither is concerned with the other's presence. But a young calf is recognized as crocodile prey by both, and a hippo's attitude toward the reptiles undergoes a total reversal with the birth of her calf. The imminent appearance of a threat to her calf galvanized the old hippo from her somnolent state to knife-edged vigilance. She turned to face the reed bed, her circulatory system now carrying adrenaline to all her organs. The calf, which had submerged to nurse, was jostled by the mother's movement and further disappointed when the big hippo moved to place herself between the baby itself and the reeds. Had her attention not been fastened on the snout that now came hurtling from the reeds to expose a tapered head, armored trunk, and serrated tail, the mother hippo might have noticed the otter's underwater approach and in her agitation hurled herself upon him. Samaki, however, had reached the animals undetected. He dove deeper, passing under the calf's clumsy head, but his tail brushed the ponderous buttock of the mother. With surprising agility the behemoth whirled, savaged the water where the otter had been with chops of her massive jaws, then finding nothing there, dipped her head beneath the surface in search. She saw the dimming form of the otter fading into the murky cloud of silt that drifted slowly downstream from the point of her turning and, no longer alarmed by the incident, turned again, still submerged, to face the real danger.

The crocodile spied the enormous bulk of the hippo, braked abruptly, and hung indecisively where he stopped. He noticed the lesser form of the calf partially revealed behind the cow. Although no reasoning played itself out in his small brain, the crocodile recognized the calf as food, many times the volume of what he had been chasing. A new anticipation sparked within him, but simultaneously its antithesis sprang to life. Some half a century of accumulated experience warned him that a large hippo in the vicinity of one of manageable size was to be avoided. A long-healed gash on the left side of his chest had impressed that datum in his memory more than two decades before, and that memory was enough to override his interest in the small animal.

The contretemps had given Samaki time to flash far enough away from his pursuer to break the chase. His nose was running, and from his eyes tear fluid mingled with the water still in the fur of his face. A state of high anxiety kept him in its grip. Cringing in the hollow under a riverbank root, the otter's body tried to make itself as small as possible. He never witnessed the deliberate backwatering of the crocodile or its slow movement upstream away from the hippos.

In time, the crocodile came to a halt again. And he waited.

Downstream, huddled in the bank, Samaki waited, too, but it was a very different kind of waiting.

Hours passed. Upstream the crocodile emerged from the water to bask. Further downstream the crocodile's mate hung immobile in the river; several of her young rested on her trunk and tail as if on some submerged timber. Samaki awakened from a fitful sleep, no longer quite exhausted, but not yet fully recovered from his encounter. His nose was dry again. And the tears no longer flowed. The crocodile had become only a nebulous memory, all but dormant in his brain, but only dormant. Samaki had learned several lessons that might mean the difference between surviving and dying another day. He knew now that dodging around obstacles worked. He knew that sudden changes of course could gain distance and time for him. He knew that a hippo with a calf were to be avoided, but that if necessary they could provide unwitting protection. And he knew, too, from harrowing experience now superimposed on the instinctive knowledge, that a large crocodile was to be avoided at all cost. The lessons were waiting, in storage, in the higher centers of his brain, but they had also been entered into the memory that lay within his muscles and the purely reactive loci of his nervous system. His movements in a similar predicament would be surer, more automatic. An otter learns quickly and indelibly.

Samaki yawned and stretched, and in so doing became aware of a soreness in muscles of the back that had been exercised to their limits; no pursuit of a fish had ever been bound to such urgency. He peered warily from behind the roots, listened intently, and took in air through flared nostrils. No hint of danger came to him. He slipped into the water, looked, listened, and sniffed again, then turned to the bank and pulled himself out onto land. He surveyed the landscape before him, then turned again to scan the river. Satisfied at last, he made his way inland to where brush would permit him to travel under cover while keeping an eye on the relatively barren floodbed.

A quarter of an hour later his route brought him to a small tributary, where a frog squatted on a mudbank. The frog catapulted from its resting place into the stream, but Samaki, from a combination of practice and inborn aptitude, predicted its trajectory, leaped toward the landing point, and hit the shallow water inches behind the creature. A puff of silt told him where the frog had gone, and it was his. He carried it to shore, held it, its legs still twitching spasmodically, and ate it. Only then, as he rummaged around in search of other fare, did he catch the scents on the bank that he recognized as those of two of the cubs. He sensed that something was absent, and this disquieted him vaguely, but that the missing element was the scent of the second female cub eluded him. In his flight he had not witnessed the death of the cub, and in time he would forget her completely.

He did recall, however, and clearly, his earlier meeting with the cubs and the romp that had been so satisfying. So it was that the prospect of pleasurable company turned his steps upstream along the creek. The trail, as any otter's will, ended often at the water's edge, to be continued elsewhere as a haze of scent on an exposed rock, to disappear again, and reappear farther along on the shore. Samaki's quest was an unhurried one, in part because of the discontinuity of the trail, and in part because his own travels tended to follow the same interrupted intinerary studded with interesting side excursions and the happy distractions of stumbling adventitiously onto small, edible kinds of water life.

Further on, the forest gave way to a clearing through which the brook flowed. Here Samaki's wariness emerged again, for he could detect a splashing in the water too loud to have been made by anything small enough to eat. But there was in the sound an element of the familiar, something that said, "Come." Then it was punctuated by a single sharp chirp; Samaki's memories crystallized. Not only was the chirp an otter's, but the voice was the male cub's. Samaki answered with two shrill syllables of his own, and in answer the two cubs bounded into sight. They paused briefly before the adult, who touched his nose to each of them, verifying their identity conclusively; the cubs were young enough not to feel the need for such protocol, for at their age any otter of any size is welcome company. They had held motionless for the grown otter's inspection; now that

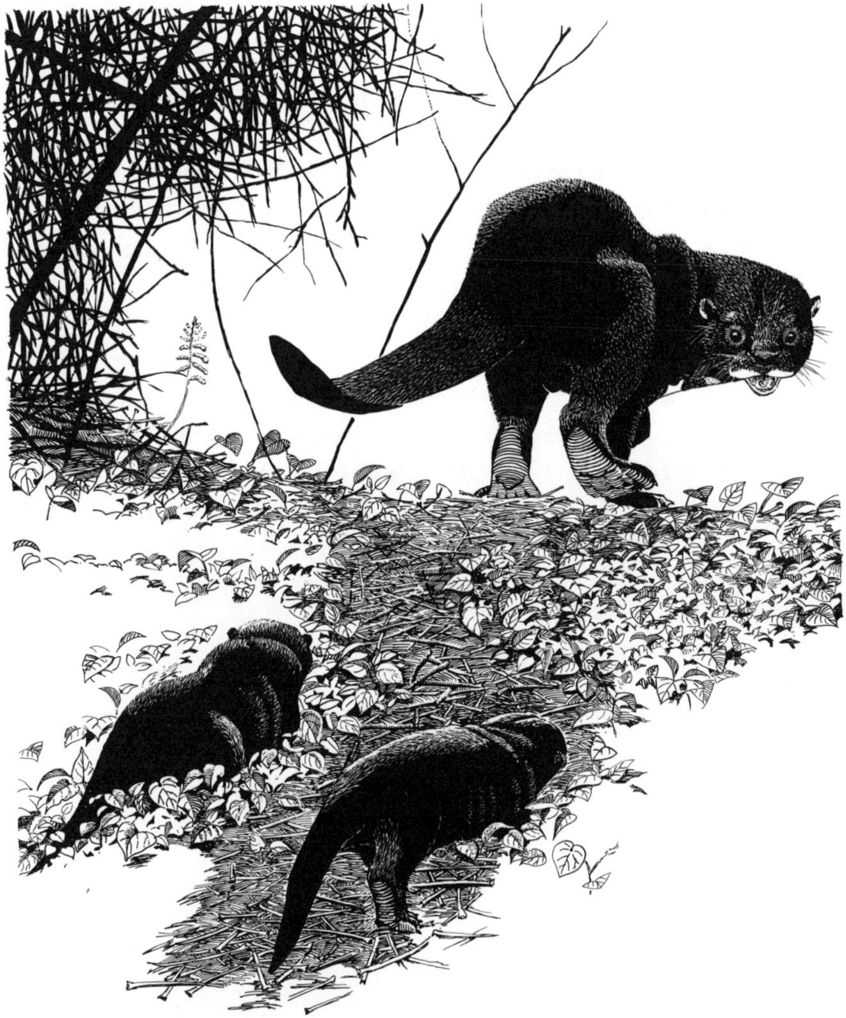

it was done, both cubs leaped upon Samaki, biting and worrying at the loose folds of his skin. He replied in kind, but softened his bite appropriately—most of the time. Samaki may not have been aware of it, but the cubs had attached themselves to more than his skin. When the scuffling ended they would follow him, and although he could not look consciously toward the future, his joy in their company made it clear that he would not merely tolerate them, but welcome their presence until time loosened the bonds on the part of the cubs and they yielded to the urge for independent lives. No mother otter would have permitted a male to associate with cubs so young, but nature had brought the males of the species farther along toward parenthood than the females realized. Fartherhood had been thrust upon Samaki. He was ready.

AUTHOR'S NOTE

Samaki is a spot-necked otter, *Hydrictis maculicollis*. If you look in the recent literature of mammalogy, you will find the species listed as *Lutra maculicollis*, on the mistaken premise that, because it resembles such species as the North American and Eurasian otters, superficially it must be closely related to them. My own studies of the anatomy and behavior of otters, however, have indicated unmistakably that the spot-neck shares characteristics with both the *Lutra* otters and with the larger group of species that embrace the clawless otters, sea otter, and giant otter, and that it probably evolved earlier than other extant species. The clawless otter, Mkono, belongs to the species *Aonyx capensis*. Both of Africa's otter species are found locally throughout the non-desert areas of that continent. Unfortunately, virtually no information exists about the number of otters that still inhabit Africa; considering how the otters of Europe and the United States have shrunk in number under our very eyes, but almost unnoticed, the future of Africa's otters is far from secure. And all for fur coats!

Samaki's story is fiction, but I have taken pains to ground it as solidly as I know how in the observed behavior of the animals portrayed. Some of what the otters of *Samaki* do is based on what I have watched captive spot-necks do, and a little springs from my observations, over eighteen years, of otters of other species from North and South America, Europe, and Asia. Of these latter activities I have incorporated only such as my studies have shown me are common to many species and are likely to be parts of the repertoire of spot-necked otters, as well. I am confident that I have introduced nothing that will prove to be alien to the spot-necks.

Most of the individual otters in the story are based on animals I have known. Samaki, as an older cub and adult, is patterned on an otter whose name was the same; he lived with me in my home for some seven years, and some of his real life I have already narrated in *Beever & Company*, including his willingness to adopt an otter of another species as a playmate. His acceptance, in his waning years, of a new young male is the source of the character of Mzee.

Samaki's early cubhood comes from several cubs, most of them reared by their mother, but including two I had to raise by hand. The swimming lessons and Maji's behavior toward her mate derive largely from observations of these animals, which, so far as I can ascertain, are the only spot-necks ever to have bred outside Africa.

Mkono is, in part, an African clawess otter cub named Joey, who also appeared in *Beever & Company*, and in part several small-clawed otters. This latter Asian species is, behaviorally and in its life style, very much like the larger African clawless, and I have no qualms about having extrapolated from my knowledge of its behavior to portray the clawless otters.

On one matter I am on less firm ground. Very little information exists that provides us with any idea of the size of the home territory of the spot-necked otter in the wild. Observations by M. A. E. Mortimer in 1963, and by G. D. H. Carpenter much earlier, indicate that in bays of Lake Victoria, where human pressure is minimal and food species are plentiful, the otters may live in some numbers, sharing the hunting waters and showing little territorial behavior. In places less bounteous the otters are believed to behave in a less tolerant way toward one another, for they have nowhere else been reported to be seen in numbers. Because so many other aspects of the behavior of otters are common to many species, I have based the territorial spacing and wanderings of Samaki and his kin on the careful studies of the Eurasian otter in Sweden, made by Sam Erlinge, with adjustments to allow for the difference in climatic conditions between the seasonally ice-bound northern lands and the relatively even climate along a permanently flowing East African river. Future field study may show this aspect of Samaki's story to be less accurate than the specific social behavior depicted, but there was no way for me to fudge on the matter, and I have chosen to make the best guess I could.

A few other incidents deserve brief explanation. Samaki's "attack" on the tip of the elephant's trunk has its origin in an unfortunate incident that took place in a zoo. A Eurasian otter, through human error, escaped from her enclosure and lived at large for some days before she was recaptured. In that time, she killed two flamingos. The otter would not have attacked birds of such size had she perceived them in their entirety; in both cases she bit the heads as the flamingos held them partly submerged in their pool, sieving water through their beaks. I transmuted the birds into an elephant because, although flamingos are abundant in parts of East Africa, they are found in soda lakes where the high alkalinity does not support fish life and which, therefore, would not be frequented by otters.

Samaki's tasting of the dung beetles' ball of elephant manure may seem improbable. In the story he was to have given an expression of disgust after sniffing it, and to gain details of his reaction I decided to run a modest experiment. I worked at the time in the North Carolina Zoo, where we had no elephant, and I presented one of my otters with a ball of rhino manure instead. Dung beetles and other connoisseurs of coprology may be aware of the differences between elephant and rhino dung, but in their gross aspects the two are not dissimilar. I was totally unprepared for the otter's behavior toward the stuff, but I recorded the event, and its essence appears in the story.

The mongoose and pill millipede episode springs from some experiments done by Dr. Thomas Eisner and me at the Bronx Zoo. Our report in *Science* was objected to by some who felt that the mongoose's behavior was an artifact of captivity. (Such objections are almost always ill-founded, for anyone familiar with animals can usually distinguish easily between natural behaviors and those induced by captive conditions.) After the objections appeared in print, another reader cited an old South African book, unknown to Eisner and me, in which the author described watching a wild, free mongoose opening a pill millipede in the fashion we described.

The behavior of the pouched rat is based on other observations I made at the Bronx Zoo, which are described more fully in *Animal Kingdom* (1959). The account of the actions of the protective hippo female derives from my experiences with zoo hippos and from published reports of field observers. The bulk of the behavior of the crocodiles outlined in the story is based on the published field observations of Hugh B. Cott and of Anthony Pooley; the final chase of Samaki by the male crocodile is, of necessity, wholly made up. I have not been able to determine how fast a big crocodile can swim, so I gave Samaki a good lead. The otter's evasive actions, however, are well within what I believe are the capabilities of that species.

Throughout the narrative I have borrowed, too, from scattered references to spot-necked and clawless otters and from observations made in recent years by Dr. David Rowe-Rowe of South Africa. On one point I have chosen to depart from the field observations, however, and hope Dave will not think unkindly of me for it. Mkono is more diurnal than the clawless otters in Rowe-Rowe's experience; I have made this change because my own clawless otter cub, Joey, was active only by day and because other species of otters, which are normally quite active by day, become largely nocturnal where human activity is high.

Samaki's adventure with the electric catfish owes something to my own literally first-hand experience with the species. When I was in college I visited the New York Aquarium at its temporary quarters in the Bronx Zoo Lion

House. There, behind the scenes, the late Christopher Coates, its director, insisted that I heft "the world's heaviest fish," which he proffered to me in a net. The jolt that went through me I will never quite forget, and I never again let Coates sucker me into another of his practical jokes when later we were colleagues. Dr. James Atz of the American Museum of Natural History helped me add to the authenticity of the electric catfish sequence and was of great help in finding specimens of appropriate fish species for the illustrations. I am grateful, too, to Dr. Philippe Falkenberg of Wake Forest University, who found for me scientific papers dealing with the physical responses of laboratory animals to electric shock. These papers are the basis of the otter's behavior, with a few modifications to allow for the fact that Samaki received his shock while under water.

Further thanks are due to those who have in one way or another helped me take care of the spot-necked otters over the years: Scott Becker, my young otter sitter over the years, and to Aleine York and the other keepers of the North Carolina Zoo who were such excellent caretakers and observers during our time there.

One next to final note: The Mazingira River is a composite of several East African rivers. The zoologist in Chapter 12 is, as might be guessed, me. The ultimate fate of the film cannister is fictional, but there *is* a deteriorating cartridge of film somewhere along the banks of the Awash River in Ethiopia, and it did hold the latent images of an otter footprint.

My last task is to absolve those mentioned above for their help of any complicity if I have distorted their data and misportrayed the creatures in my story. I thank, too, all the otters who have been my subjects and my tutors over the years. I have tried to depict them as I believe them to be and to feel. When it is my time to cross the River Styx, I hope I will be met in midstream by the real Samaki and that he will not disapprove of my efforts to show his personality as it was and his life as it might have been.

J.A.D.   Brookfield, Ill.

ABOUT THE AUTHOR

JOSEPH A. DAVIS is Superintendent of Mammals at Chicago's Brookfield Zoo and Honorary Consultant to the Survival Service Commission of the International Union for the Conservation of Nature in the Otter Specialist Group. Previously he has been general curator of the North Carolina Zoological Park and before that spent sixteen years at the New York Zoological Society as Curator of Mammals, Scientific Assistant to the Director, and a Field Associate in Mammalogy. He has kept at home or studied in the wild most of the world's species of otter and, indeed, this novel is based on his research. His books include *Beever & Company, 500 Animals from A to Z, Pandas,* and the text for Nina Leen's photographs in *And Then There Were None.*